IMPERIAL AUSTRIA

IMPERIAL AUSTRIA

TREASURES OF
ART, ARMS & ARMOR
FROM THE STATE OF STYRIA

by PETER KRENN

and WALTER J. KARCHESKI, JR.

Coordinated by KATHERINE S. HOWE

PRESTEL

Imperial Austria: Treasures of Art, Arms & Armor from the State of Styria was published in conjunction with the exhibition organized by the Museum of Fine Arts, Houston in collaboration with the Fine Arts Museums of San Francisco, the Smithsonian Institution and the IBM Gallery of Science and Art, held at:

The Fine Arts Museums of San Francisco, M.H. de Young Memorial Museum, San Francisco
February 22–May 17, 1992

The IBM Gallery of Science and Art, New York City
June 30–August 22, 1992

The Smithsonian Institution, International Gallery, Washington, D.C.
October 3, 1992–January 24, 1993

The Museum of Fine Arts, Houston
March 14–June 27, 1993

The objects in the exhibition were graciously lent by the Government for the State of Styria/ Austria from the Steiermärkisches Landesmuseum Joanneum in Graz, Austria and other private lenders.

Imperial Austria: Treasures of Art, Arms & Armor from the State of Styria was sponsored by Swarovski. In Houston and San Francisco, this exhibition was funded in part by the National Endowment for the Arts, a federal agency. Lufthansa German Airlines provided international transportation for this exhibition.

Prestel-Verlag, Mandlstrasse 26, D-8000 Munich 40, Germany
Tel: (89) 38 17 09 0; Fax: (89) 38 17 09 35

Distributed in continental Europe by Prestel-Verlag
Verlegerdienst München GmbH & Co Kg
Gutenbergstrasse 1, D-8031 Gilching, Germany
Tel: (8105) 21 10; Fax: (8105) 55 20

Distributed in the USA and Canada by te Neues Publishing Company,
15 East 76th Street, New York, NY 10021, USA
Tel: (212) 288 0265; Fax: (212) 570 2373

Distributed in Japan by YOHAN-Western Publications Distribution
Agency, 14-9 Okubo 3-chome, Sinjuku-ku, J-Tokyo 169
Tel: (3) 208 0181; Fax: (3) 209 0288

Distributed in the United Kingdom, Ireland and all remaining
countries by Thames & Hudson Limited, 30-40 Bloomsbury Street,
London WC1B 3 QP, England
Tel: (71) 636 5488; Fax: (71) 636 4799

Designed by Staples & Charles Ltd/Theresa W. Grate
Edited by Mary Christian
Typeset in Trajan and Berkeley Book
Color separations by Merk + Steitz GmbH, Villingen-Schwenningen, Germany
Printed by Peradruck Matthias, Gräfelfing, Germany
Bound by R. Oldenbourg, Heimstetten, Germany

Printed in Germany

ISBN 3-7913-1139-5

Cover:
Michel Witz the Younger,
Black-and-White Three-quarter
Armor for a Nobleman, c. 1550
[checklist no. 95].

Frontispiece:
Danube School, Panel from the
Miraculous Altar of Mariazell,
1512 [checklist no. 59].

CONTENTS

DIRECTORS' FOREWORD

In 1988 Annelie Hochkofler, Special Envoy from the State of Styria to the United States, met Peter C. Marzio of the Museum of Fine Arts, Houston and Tom L. Freudenheim of the Smithsonian Institution. Dr. Hochkofler told them about her state's remarkable history as a European bulwark against the Ottoman Empire and the way the Ottoman challenge has permeated Styrian art and history for more than two hundred years. She also described a unique survivor from this era, the Landeszeughaus, the extraordinary Renaissance armory located in the Styrian city of Graz. Containing more than thirty-two thousand objects dating from the late Gothic through the Baroque periods, it is the oldest and largest surviving armory in the Western world, yet its rare collection and the history and the art associated with it are largely unknown in the United States. When Peter Marzio and Tom Freudenheim learned that for the first time in its history the State of Styria would consider lending its rare art and armor collections, they saw the possibility for an extraordinary American exhibition. Soon thereafter Richard P. Berglund of the IBM Gallery of Science and Art and Harry S. Parker of the Fine Arts Museums of San Francisco joined the project and *Imperial Austria: Treasures of Art, Arms & Armor from the State of Styria* was born.

The exhibition and this publication are truly as unique as the armor and art that inspired them. The exhibition has been a model of international cooperation. The Styrian government under Governor Dr. Joseph Krainer and the Joanneum, the Styrian state museum that is the principal lender to the exhibition, have unfailingly supported this complex project and have done so with efficiency, professionalism, generosity, and grace. Although numerous Styrians were crucial to the project, Annelie Hochkofler and Peter Krenn deserve special recognition for their tireless effort and diligence. In North America the exhibition is the result of dedicated work by a consortium of institutions working in partnership and sharing expertise. Both the book and the exhibition have been greatly enhanced by this shared effort and teamwork. Walter J. Karcheski, Jr., consulting curator for the exhibition, designers Robert Staples and Barbara Charles, coordinating curator Katherine S. Howe, and George T.M. Shackelford have also been key participants in the project, and we cannot forget the late Leonid Tarassuk, the gifted armor curator who counseled the organizers during the exhibition's formative stages.

Lastly, the organizing institutions are deeply indebted to the Swarovski Corporation, the corporate sponsor for the exhibition, for its generous support; to Lufthansa German Airlines for transporting scholars and the exhibition to and from Graz; and to the National Endowment for the Arts, a federal agency, for its implementation grant to the exhibition.

Peter C. Marzio
The Museum of Fine Arts, Houston

Tom L. Freudenheim
Smithsonian Institution

Harry S. Parker III
The Fine Arts Museums
of San Francisco

Richard P. Berglund
IBM Gallery of Science and Art

THE LANDESZEUGHAUS GRAZ AND ITS PLACE IN HISTORY

Peter Krenn

1
Interior View of the Landeszeughaus Graz.

The Landeszeughaus collection of more than five thousand staff weapons is stored on the fourth floor. Most of these weapons were made in Upper Austria in the 16th century.

The wooden ceilings, floors, and paneled walls all absorb moisture and keep the weapons from rusting. In addition to staff weapons, approximately twenty-four hundred swords and daggers, most of them made in Styrian workshops, are housed on this floor.

The author gratefully acknowledges Dr. Christine Rabensteiner, curator of paintings at the Alte Galerie, for her contributions to the catalogue regarding the fine art, as well as Ruth Rietz Barney, his translator.

Armories were establishments of the Renaissance that came into existence in the fifteenth century to protect a government's widening array of military weapons. Armories, or German *Zeughäuser,* were often built in connection with armament workshops, where new arms were produced and used ones repaired. At first, they served only to safeguard cannons, the largest and most expensive type of explosive weapon, and the first artillery to be widely developed after the invention of gunpowder. But at the beginning of the sixteenth century, the armory's function became less specialized; this is clear by the German term *Zeughaus,* which means a house for everything having to do with ordnance [figure 1]. From that time, the small firearms of the infantry, which were gaining new significance at a time of revolutionary change in military tactics, entered the arsenal. Over the years, the scope of the armory's collection expanded to include armor and other accoutrements of the fighting man.

The ordnance books of Emperor Maximilian I (reigned 1493–1519) at the Kunsthistorisches Museum in Vienna provide a good example of the variety of military supplies contained in a good armory. The emperor's chief master of ordnance compiled these books in about 1512, and his court painter Jörg Kölderer (active 1497–1540) illustrated them. These pictorial inventories of the armories in the emperor's hereditary provinces show heavy and light ordnance, firearms, halberds, pikes, and other weapons and war materials.

Throughout the sixteenth century, numerous armories were built with one or more upper floors to house all of the small firearms, including those of the totally re-equipped cavalry. Soon almost every fortified city in Europe had an armory; some cities, such as Graz, had more than one. Graz possessed three, which corresponded to its importance as the capital of Styria and residence of the reigning prince.

The smallest of Graz's armories was the municipal armory, which held the arms of the municipal militia and the gatekeepers. Next came the armory of the regent who would summon the mercenary troops-in-waiting to defend his province. Finally, there was the armory of the province as represented by the estates, in which ordnance for the fortified cities and border strongholds, as well as equipment for the provincial levy, was stored. This was the largest of the three and is the only surviving armory. Not only is Landeszeughaus Graz, as this is known today, one of the very few early modern armories still in existence anywhere, but its original buildings and its inventory, amassed over the course of three centuries, are also intact. With its arsenal-like display, which local specialists have protected from becoming a "modern" museum, the Landeszeughaus Graz is thoroughly unique [figure 4].

STYRIA, BULWARK OF THE HOLY ROMAN EMPIRE

A summary of the geopolitical situation of Styria can explain how the

2

2
Portal of the Landeszeughaus with the Styrian Crowned Panther.

The main portal of the Zeughaus distinguishes this otherwise utilitarian storage building. The portal is crowned by a gable with the Styrian panther and is flanked by monumental figures of Mars and Minerva. These statues, carved by the Italian sculptor Giovanni Marmolo, are the earliest examples of monumental Baroque art in Styria.

3
Exterior View of the
Landeszeughaus Graz.

The five-story facade on the left
was designed in 1642–44 by
the architect Antonio Solario.
The adjacent Renaissance-style
building, the Landhaus, was
erected in 1557–65 by Domenio
dell'Allio of Lugano. The
Landhaus was, and still is, the
seat of the Styrian government.

Landeszeughaus collection evolved. As its German name (*Steiermark*—
literally, a border defense region) reveals, Styria originated as a borderland
[figure 5]. Along with several other such lands, it formed a protective
belt stretching from the Baltic to the Adriatic that, from the tenth century
on, protected this area of German settlement and culture against attacks
from the East. The varied topographical features of the land played an
important role in shaping Styria's development. While the north of Styria
is secured by the Alps, the rest of the land is composed of Alpine foothills
that drop off toward the east. Since the border is totally open, it offers no
natural protection. Furthermore, for a thousand years, the favorable
living conditions of this eastern approach to Styria, the so-called
Pannonian plain (essentially today's Hungary and northeastern
Yugoslavia), attracted the aggressive horse cultures from the steppes of

Eurasia. Styria emerged in this eastern border area as a bulwark and front line of a German Empire constantly threatened by invasion. Its duty was to prevent intruders from penetrating into the Alpine area, thus protecting the southern flank of Vienna and of the Danube valley, which forms the main passageway to central Europe.

For this reason, Styria has always contained numerous fortresses and other defensive installations, which is why it was sometimes called the "land of a thousand fortresses." In 1180 Styria became a duchy, which stabilized its exterior borders as well as its interior structure, and from 1282 it belonged to the Habsburgs. Originally the Habsburgs came from the west; their ancestral regions lay in northern Switzerland and on the upper Rhine. In the second half of the thirteenth century, however, under the leadership of Rudolph I (reigned 1273–1291), the dynasty's first German king, they defeated the king of Bohemia and Moravia and definitively shifted their residence to Vienna, the chief city of the Eastern Empire (Austria). The duchies of Austria (Upper and Lower Austria),

4

4
Interior View of the Fourth Floor in the Landeszeughaus Graz.

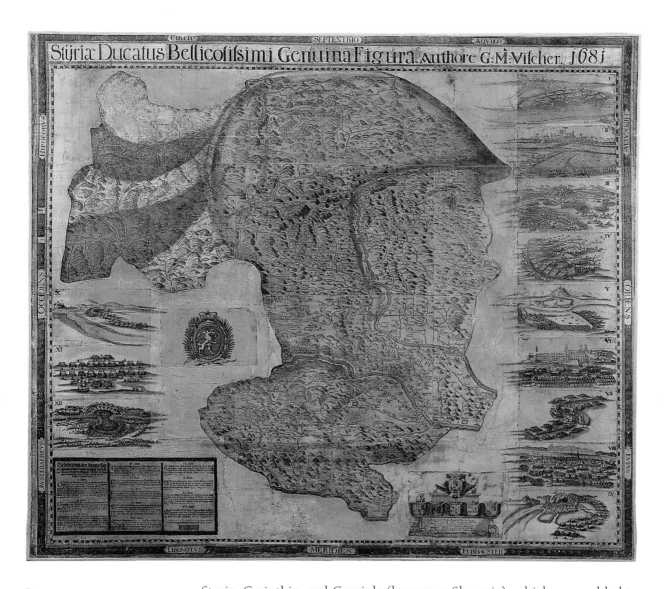

5
Georg Matthäus Vischer, *Map of Styria formed as the Head of Mars, God of War,* 1681 [checklist no. 51].

As this map of Styria as Mars demonstrates, Styria recognized its position as a defensive bulwark for Eastern Europe.

Styria, Carinthia, and Carniola (known as Slovenia), which were added to their domains as crown lands at that time, became the consolidated base from which they built their future position as the most powerful dynasty in Europe. Eventually, they not only ruled over a large number of central European peoples, but also held the prestigious office of emperor of the entire German nation. On the other hand, it was precisely these crown lands that tested the Habsburg resources when it became necessary for the nation to defend itself against the Ottoman Turks, who began to push northward into the Balkans in the fourteenth century.

The armaments in the Landeszeughaus were accumulated primarily during the period when Styria fought to defend the Habsburg lands from the Ottoman threat. The Ottoman Empire was a traditional military empire of conquest, made more frightening to Europeans because it was at the same time an Islamic state [figure 6]. It took the Ottomans more than one hundred years from when they first crossed into Europe from

Anatolia to conquer Byzantium, the last remnant of the Roman Empire, and to focus directly on lands that bordered the Habsburg realm. In the fifteenth century, Ottoman military forces were perhaps the best in Europe. They used state-of-the-art artillery to reduce the walls of Constantinople in 1453. Their well-coordinated forces—consisting of an armed cavalry called *spahis;* a disciplined and well-trained corps of professionals called *Janissaries;* and large numbers of irregulars and other forces—easily crushed the medieval Balkan states as well as several major crusades sent by the Europeans. At the height of the period of Ottoman expansion, the sultan himself led his armies out of Istanbul each spring for the annual campaign. The most powerful Ottoman ruler, Süleyman the Magnificent (reigned 1520–1566), led his armies in numerous campaigns into Habsburg lands in the first half of the sixteenth century, capturing Belgrade in 1521, killing the Hungarian and Bohemian king at Mohács in 1526, and trying to conquer Vienna itself in 1529 and 1532. Süleyman could not take Vienna, but he did incorporate most of Hungary into his empire and made Transylvania his vassal state. The Ottomans ruled these lands near Styria for more than one hundred and fifty years.

The impact of the Ottoman campaign on the exposed Habsburg periphery was serious. Styria especially suffered at the hands of mounted irregulars, which it first encountered in 1471. An attack in August 1480 by a force of sixteen thousand of these irregulars, at a time when the Styrian estates were involved in a war with Hungary, led to widespread destruction. The partially preserved *Plague of God* fresco on the south side of the Graz cathedral commemorates this disaster by comparing its effects to those of plagues of locusts and disease ravaging the land.

The devastating consequences of inadequate defenses against the Ottomans, and the lesson that they could not rely on imperial mercenaries, convinced the Styrian estates they would have to strengthen their indigenous forces. In 1480 they assembled in Graz and decided to require each landlord to provide one armed horseman for every one hundred guilders of annual income. This new system supplemented the existing practice of drafting every tenth man on foot and provided six to seven hundred horses. Later, the estates employed mercenaries instead. Even if no concrete evidence exists to prove it, we can assume that the beginning of a provincial arms depot dates to those years at the close of the fifteenth century.

We begin to find documentary evidence about armaments during the era of Emperor Maximilian I, who made far-reaching efforts to secure his hereditary provinces. He held the provinces to treaties of assistance that obliged them to provide mutual support in the case of war. Maximilian also initiated the buildup of a modern armaments industry and saw to it that a sufficient supply of weapons was stored in the newly constructed arsenals. Nonetheless, he was unable to realize his ambitious plan to defeat the Ottomans decisively in a large-scale pincer attack from the Balkans and North Africa. Of significance for Styria was his active interest in the production of forged-iron field guns and heavy harquebuses by the Upper Styrian gunmaking concern, Pögl. Maximilian supported this firm with several large commissions and provided the necessary resources to improve the technique for boring gun barrels, allowing him to standardize the caliber of his artillery. He also helped to modernize the armorer's craft in Styria by summoning the outstanding master Hans Maystetter (active 1508–1533) from Innsbruck to Graz [figure 12]. Today the armory still owns three forged-iron light field guns (falconets), several heavy harquebuses, and eight fluted suits of armor from those early years of Styrian defense against the Ottomans.

SECURING THE FRONTIER

Maximilian's successor, Emperor Ferdinand I (named Archduke of Austria 1521, Emperor 1556–64), was the one who felt the full brunt of Süleyman the Magnificent's onslaught. He was able to repel the sultan before he reached Vienna in 1529 and 1532, but after each of these failed attacks, Ottoman forces turned southward across eastern Styria, leaving a path of devastation. To prevent further plundering, Ferdinand ordered the refortification of the most endangered Styrian cities following the model of the Italian bastion system. He secured Italian builders familiar with the Renaissance style, and thus Graz was fortified in 1544 with the "Schlossberg" by Domenico dell'Allio of Lugano (d. 1563) [figure 7]. Dell'Allio also built the palace in the Herrengasse for the Styrian estates and thereby strongly influenced Styrian palace construction in the sixteenth century. He was responsible for the fortification of the Styrian cities of Fürstenfeld, Radkersburg [figure 9], and Marburg on the Drava as well.

8

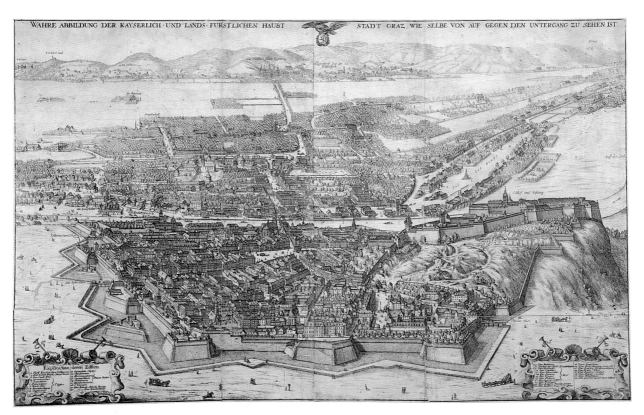

In order to intercept and counter Ottoman advances before they reached any vital zones, Ferdinand created a new buffer, the so-called military frontier, which swept across the southern parts of modern Croatia between the Adriatic Sea and the Drava River. Fortresses, forts, and watchtowers were built along the frontier, provided with artillery, and settled with refugees from the Ottoman areas of Serbia and Bosnia [figures 8, 9, 10]. In return for their military service in the frontier region, these settlers received important privileges, including freedom from ordinary taxes. The Styrian estates concerned themselves especially with the eastern sector of the military between the Sava and the Drava Rivers. Since this area was considered the frontline of Styria, they expanded the city of Varazdin, seat of the border commandant, to a garrison, a task also given

7
Andreas Trost, *View of City and Fortress of Graz,* 1703 [checklist no. 52].

This is one of the best historical views of Graz. While the west side of the city is secured by the river Mur, the other three sides are surrounded by fortifications that follow the model of the Italian bastion system. On top of the hill is the distinctive watchtower of Graz and the fortress containing barracks, armsmakers' workshops, and a prisoners' dungeon.

8, 9, 10
Georg Matthäus Vischer, *Castle of Thalberg*, the *Fortified City of Radkersburg*, and *Castle of Riegersburg* from *Topographia Ducatus Stiriae*, 1681 [checklist no. 53].

These fortified places are situated strategically along the eastern border of the country. Thalberg is the oldest, dating from the 12th century. The two towers, the palace, and the exterior walls date from the Romanesque period.

10

to dell'Allio. They also fortified the Slávonic towns of Kopreinitz, St. Georgen, Kreuz, and Ibanitz, thus securing this sector.

During this period of vastly increased military preparedness, the Landeszeughaus in Graz assumed a well-defined role as the central arsenal of the estates. By 1547, an armskeeper had been hired to maintain and manage the war materials, which had increased considerably in less than a decade. The earliest preserved inventory, from 1557, lists 19,400 items, including ammunition. At first, the objects were housed in diverse arms sheds and vaults in the area of the provincial palace and the city gates. With the construction of the Renaissance palace in 1557–65, however, most of the inventory was moved to its spacious attic rooms.

ARCHDUKE KARL II AND GRAZ

After the death of Ferdinand I in 1564, his empire was divided among his sons. Archduke Karl II (reigned 1564–1590) [figures 13, 14] received the complex of regions known as Inner Austria, which consisted of the imperial duchies of Styria, Carinthia, and Carniola, as well as Gorizia, Trieste, and parts of Friuli in northern Italy. He made Graz his capital and residence, since the city's good fortification and existing official structures were the most advanced of his lands. Since Inner Austria was now dissociated from the rest of the Austrian hereditary provinces and it now had to rely on itself for protection, Karl and the estates undertook still more defense-related projects. In 1566 and again in 1575, they sought advice from the imperial chief field marshal, Lazarus von Schwendi. In his report "Advice on How to Wage War against the Turks,"

12
Hans Maystetter, Field Armor of the "Maximilian" form, 1510–11 [checklist no. 60].

This is the only armor of this type at the Landeszeughaus that can be attributed to a specific maker. Hans Maystetter, whose mark appears on the left pauldron, was first recorded in Innsbruck in 1508 and was called to Graz in 1510 at the emperor's command.

von Schwendi proposed reducing the number of recruited mercenaries and training more of the provinces' own vassals and nobility. In the following years, a strong arms buildup began. Weapons were produced in native workshops and acquired from abroad, usually from the German arms centers of Nuremberg, Augsburg, and Suhl. As a result, in only a few years the armory possessed an enormous supply of weapons.

STYRIAN TROOPS AND THEIR WEAPONS

During the second half of the sixteenth century, Styrian forces were divided into infantry and cavalry, and each bore specialized equipment. Three types of soldiers fought on foot. The first were the harquebusiers, of whom the landed lords had to raise twenty-five hundred. The harque-busier wore a marksman's helmet and carried a wheel-lock gun as his main weapon. At the end of the sixteenth century, musketeers were added as a second infantry element [figure 63]. The musketeer wore no protective armor and fought with a wheel-lock or matchlock musket, which had to be fired from a rest because of its weight. In addition to these troops bearing firearms, there were pikemen, known as *Knechte* or later *Pikeniere*. They fought with ten- to twelve-foot-long pikes and protected the musketeers while they reloaded during cavalry attacks. *Knechte* wore infantry armor consisting of a burgonet, an almain collar, a breastplate with tassets, and a backplate.

The cavalry also consisted of three parts. The first division, and the best to combat the quick Ottoman horsemen, were the harquebusier-riders, who combined maneuverability with firepower. They were the most frequently used force during the so-called long war against the Ottomans from 1593 to 1606. These riders, equipped with two or three pistols, wore a burgonet (superseded in the seventeenth century by the *Zischägge*) and a bulletproof cuirass with mail sleeves. The second type of cavalry were the hussars, recruited from Croatia and Hungary, who were more lightly armed with a Hungarian-style *Zischägge*, a laminated cuirass, and a mail shirt [figure 15]. They fought with sabers and estocs and were well-suited for surprise raids and reconnaissance. Finally, there was the heavy cavalry (cuirassiers) with complete armor, which included the close helmet and cuirass, arm defenses, and leg armor that extended at least to the knee [figure 18]. As a rule, each was armed with a cavalry sword and two pistols. Only a few lancers remained among heavy cavalry, since this antiquated art of fighting, which demanded much practice, lost popularity with the nobility and fell entirely out of use in the early seventeenth

13
Martino Rota, *Portrait of Arch-duke Karl II of Inner Austria,* 1576 [checklist no. 70].

Martino Rota, a court artist in Vienna, depicted Karl II wearing an armor similar to one made about 1563 by Anton Peffenhauser of Augsburg.

14 ▶
Unidentified artist, after an engraving by Daniel Hefner, *Funeral Procession of Karl II of Inner Austria,* [checklist nos. 71.1–.6].

These paintings are copies of an extensive series of engravings that illustrates the grand funeral cortege of Archduke Karl II (1540–1590). The procession, which lasted several days, included the wide range of mourners illustrated here—close relatives, members of the court, aristocrats, and even citizens and servants.

century. In open battle, lancers were able to penetrate their opponents' ranks and throw them from their horses with the momentum of their attacks. In small skirmishes on difficult terrain, however, they lost effectiveness. All of these variations in armaments used in the Ottoman wars of the sixteenth and seventeenth centuries can still be studied uniquely in the Landeszeughaus. There, as nowhere else in Europe, is a pristine collection built by natural acquisition over the course of these dangerous centuries.

14   In 1629 the armory inventory recorded 85,000 pieces, a fourfold increase in less than seventy-five years. The existing rooms were barely able to accommodate this enormous store of arms. A German traveler who visited Graz wrote in 1632 that the Styrian estates indeed had a well-filled armory in their palace, but unfortunately everything was much too cramped and jumbled. A few years later, in order to remedy this situation, which was, after all, a threat to civil defense, the estates decided to construct a spacious armory. They commissioned the southern Swiss master builder Antonio Solario (d. 1672), who lived in Graz. He erected the new building between 1642 and 1644, connecting it directly to the palace [figure 3]. It was a sober, five-story building whose unadorned 132-foot-long side facing a courtyard made it look like a warehouse. The building's noble character is revealed only by the narrow, towering entrance facade that faces the Herrengasse. The entrance's striking early Baroque rustic portal [figure 2]; its crowned panther, symbol of the province; and the flanking monumental statues of the ancient gods of war, Mars and Minerva, are the building's only artistic embellishments.

LIFE AT THE FRONTIER

With the Peace of Zsitvatorok, which ended the "long war" in 1606, hostilities between the Habsburg and Ottoman empires virtually ceased. The Ottomans became engaged against the Poles, the Persians, and the Venetians, while imperial forces were entangled in the Thirty Years' War, which plagued Europe from 1618 to 1648. Had the Ottomans executed a significant attack on Vienna during this period, the city would certainly have fallen. But, by this time, the Ottoman Empire had begun its slow decline and formal hostilities remained limited to a small border war of local origin. Despite the lull in fighting the sultan, Styria's military efforts did not come to a standstill. The most common military events of this period were the frequent incursions of the so-called *Tschettieren* (from the Croatian *ceta,* or armed band), in which small groups led raids across the

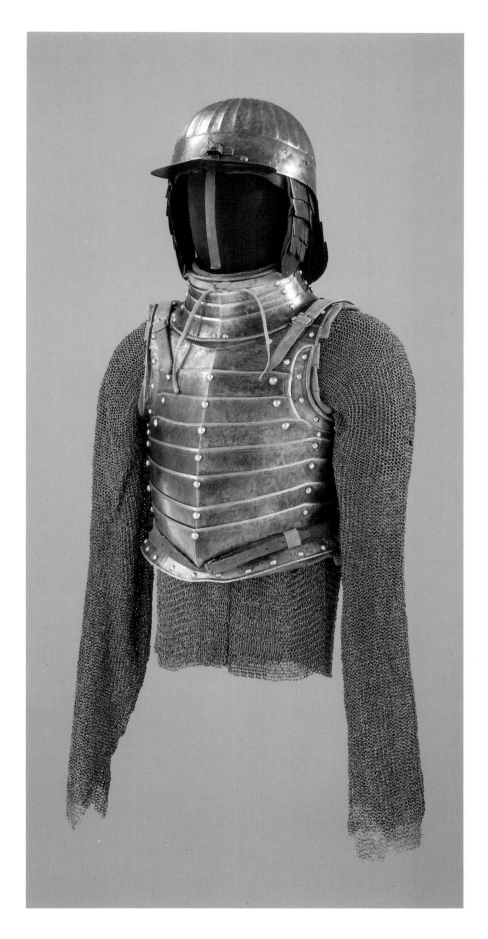

15
Armor for a Hussar: Cuirass,
Mail Shirt, and Hungarian-style
Helmet (*Zischägge*), 1590–1600
[checklist nos. 177.1–.3].

16, 17
From Jacob Jacques de Gheyn,
Waffenhandlung von den Roren,
Musquetten undt Spiessen, 1607
[checklist no. 234].

This popular book contained
weapons drills for the pikeman,
the musketeer, and the harque-
busier. It was illustrated by
de Gheyn, a Netherlandish
designer, engraver, and painter.

border, often to abduct people and livestock. The mutual sale and repur-
chase of prisoners flourished, as did the sale of Christian children to the
Ottomans. In fact, a new arms boom began in 1619 when Gábor Bethlen,
Prince of Transylvania and an ally of the Ottomans, rose up against the
emperor and marched on Vienna. He wanted to conquer the Inner
Austrian provinces, but failed to do so. Nonetheless, fearing an invasion
from Bethlen, the Styrian government put twelve hundred footmen and
several hundred musketeers and harquebusier-riders in place, and the
armory received a new wave of armaments. These weapons were largely
based on the western European and Dutch models that had originated in
the military reform of Prince Maurice of Orange. The designs became
known in Styria through an illustrated drill book published in 1607, in
which Maurice's employee, Jacob Jacques de Gheyn (1565–1629), illustrated the new arms in detail [figures 16, 17]. The new models swept
Europe, and in Styria they inspired a flourishing local arms manufacture,
capable of producing great quantities of weapons. The large workshops
of the armorer Hans Prenner (d. 1645) in Graz, of the firearms makers
Kummer and Rhein near Graz, and of the sword fabricators of Weiz are
examples of the local producers that flourished during these years [figure
18]. Several hundred guns, muskets, and footsoldiers' armors from this
period are still housed in the Landeszeughaus.

THE DEFEAT OF THE OTTOMANS

In 1663 a major battle in Styria prepared the way for the ultimate with-
drawal of the Ottomans from central Europe. The Ottoman Grandvizier

Ahmed Köprülü marched into Hungary with a mighty army and spent the winter there. In Styria, the estates feared the worst and prepared accordingly. They called up six thousand men to secure the border, armed Graz with forty-two cannons, and built numerous trenches and other obstacles. In Vienna, Emperor Leopold I (reigned 1658–1705) also responded to the danger by assembling a large army and soliciting allies. When the Grandvizier pushed forward against Styria's eastern border in July 1664, an allied army of imperial, German, and French troops under the supreme command of Imperial Field Marshal Raimund Count Montecuccoli opposed him at Mogersdorf in the Raab Valley. In a major battle on August 1, 1664, the imperial forces gained the upper hand [figure 19]. The Ottoman army, only part of which was engaged, was by

18
Attributed to Hans Prenner, Three-quarter Armor for Heavy Cavalry, c. 1600–1635 [checklist nos. 272–277].

The horsemen, called cuirassiers, who wore these armors fought with broadswords and pistols. The effect of heavy cavalry can be compared to the military tank forces of today.

17

no means annihilated, but it suffered such great losses that Köprülü began to retreat. The final battle came barely twenty years later in 1683, when the Ottomans besieged Vienna. The Ottoman army suffered a devastating defeat by a relief army of united Habsburg and Polish forces, led by the gifted commander Duke Charles V of Lorraine (1643–1690). Within a few years the Ottomans were pushed completely out of Hungary and Transylvania [figure 20]. Styria, as well as its forward border region in Croatia, had suddenly become hinterland, at last losing contact with the enemy. The Peace of Karlowitz in 1699 established its new boundaries. Inner Austria and the military frontier had fulfilled their great duty, and so had the Landeszeughaus Graz.

These decisive events had a great impact on the armory. More than one hundred armors for cuirassiers were delivered in 1683, in addition to broadswords and wheel-lock and flintlock pistols. In 1688 the infantry was armed with the first flintlock muskets, equipped with early plug bayonets, which were pressed into the muzzle of the barrel. More than two hundred and fifty of these are still preserved. The inventory of 1699 lists the staggering total of 185,000 objects, the most ever recorded. That same year, the armory lost its position as the supply base for the military border, but it still supplied flintlock muskets for battles against rebellious Hungarians and for a few other minor campaigns.

THE PRESERVATION OF THE LANDESZEUGHAUS

From 1740 onward, the greatest problem facing the armory was not protecting Styria, but protecting its own collection. The first and most serious threat came when, in the course of reforming the military administration, Maria Theresa (reigned 1740–1780) abolished the Inner Austrian War Authority (*Kriegsstelle*) in Graz and made the Imperial War Ministry (*Hofkriegsrat*) responsible for arming and provisioning. She resolved to give up the armory entirely, and in 1749 she proposed to the estates that they relinquish all usable weapons to the war ministry and sell the obsolete arms as scrap metal. The Styrians objected and argued that in addition to its material value, the armory also had a symbolic importance, for it was dear to them as a memorial to the history of their country and to the valor of their forefathers. The wise Maria Theresa, not wanting to offend the Styrians unnecessarily, and respecting their tradition of defending the realm, allowed them to keep the armory. For the time being, the armory was saved.

◀◀ 19
Unknown German(?) painter, *The Battle of Mogersdorf*, c. 1665 [checklist no. 289].

This painting depicts the victorious moment in the 1664 Battle of Mogersdorf, in which soldiers led by the Imperial Field Marshall Montecuccoli attacked and defeated entrenched Ottoman forces. In a dramatic conclusion to this battle, many Ottomans drowned in the Raab River.

20
Hans Adam Weissenkircher, *St. Mary and St. Ruprecht Pleading for the Victory of the Christian Weapons over the Turks*, 1691 [checklist no. 190].

This altarpiece was painted for the Eggenberg family mausoleum located south of Graz in Ehrenhausen. Ruprecht had conquered the Ottomans at the Battle of Sissek in 1593. Weissenkircher, who was a student of the important German painter Johann Carl Loth, created some of the finest Austrian Baroque painting of his day.

21

Trophy Arrangement in the Zeughaus

Following a Baroque taste, arrangements such as this one conceptualized the idea of valor and bravery, but they ignored the historical accuracy and function of arms.

THE LANDESZEUGHAUS AS A HISTORICAL MONUMENT

More subtle dangers threatened the collection more or less simultaneously. In keeping with the decorative aesthetic of the late Baroque, and continuing into the nineteenth century, objects in the armory were often incorporated into artistic compositions with pyramids, columns, or large arrangements called trophies [figure 21]. Such decorative ensembles de-emphasized the craftsmanship and function of each weapon. One trophy, for example, was a representation of the imperial two-headed eagle constructed from pistols. These types of decorative arrangements adorned the armory's walls, windows, and ceilings. Another new function of the collection emerged from the practice of arbitrarily assigning to the best suits of armor the names of Styrian war heroes and rulers, even though such attributions had no historical validity. Like the taste for trophies, this practice essentially made the armory a memorial to Styrian military valor and heroism.

Although these measures changed the character of the arms and their display, the collection remained intact. Losses to the collection occurred in 1797 when, in the face of the advancing French army under Napoleon Bonaparte, the entire collection of fifty-two cannons was moved to safety in Novi Sad in Yugoslavia and later sold there to avoid the difficult transport back to Graz. Once emptied, the cannon hall on the ground floor of the armory was soon occupied by outside institutions, such as the municipal fire department and a private business, for which it became a storehouse. This hall did not return to the armory's control until 1985, and it has since been used for special exhibitions.

A further threat developed in 1840 during the Biedermeier period, when alterations to the armory were proposed. The plans for this renovation, which still exist, called for converting the four upper floors, which were thought to be too dark, into two high halls with larger windows that would admit more light and better display the objects. The promoters of this scheme, who were driven by their strong sense of contemporary taste, wanted to finance the renovations by selling those arms that could no longer be housed in the reduced exhibition space. Luckily, some farsighted individuals called attention to the importance of the original state of the building and persuaded the governing board to

22
Strong Box for Military Funds, second half of the 16th century [checklist no. 287].

This heavy iron strongbox, used to secure the funds from which troops were paid, features complex ironwork and an intricate interior locking system made up of twenty-six different mechanisms.

preserve the armory's original architecture.

Finally, during the last quarter of the nineteenth century, there grew a keen appreciation of the unique historic and symbolic value of the Landeszeughaus Graz. During this period, when a critical approach to history began to prevail, an interested public took decisive steps to restore the original character of the armory.

Several museum experts from Graz and Vienna were commissioned to remove the outdated Baroque displays—which then included no less than fifty-seven decorative weapons ensembles, mostly placed in window niches—and to reconstruct an installation that would closely approximate the seventeenth-century original. In addition, the objects, which were rusty and dirty from centuries of storage, were restored. In 1880 a comprehensive two-volume documentation of the building's history and collection was published, and in 1882 the armory was opened to the public. Finally, in 1892 the armory became part of the Styrian State Museum Joanneum, which the Habsburg Archduke Johann (1782–1859) had founded in 1811. Since then, the staffing and economic security of the Landeszeughaus has been the responsibility of the state.

Nevertheless, the twentieth century, with its two world wars, has posed still more dangers to the Landeszeughaus. The first threat came during the economically unsettled years after 1918, when international dealers tried to acquire several of the best pieces from the armory. When some individuals wanted to accept their offers in order to improve government revenues, the governing board of the Joanneum protested and was able to dissuade them from their short-sighted mistake. Finally, World War II brought new uncertainties. The armory successfully countered these dangers by completely transferring its contents to three remote Styrian country palaces. The collection suffered no losses and, with the support of the British occupation authority, the objects were returned to the armory, which reopened in April 1946.

Since then, the Landeszeughaus has enjoyed growing popularity. Its unique level of preservation, its great documentary value for the history and study of arms, and the authentic atmosphere of its rooms make the armory a fascinating place to visit, and one that is especially appealing to foreigners. Moreover, it illustrates the historical role of Styria as no other collection can. The armory's treasures document Styria's survival for more than two centuries on the imperiled southeastern flank of the old Habsburg Empire and its position as a bulwark and defensive barrier against the Ottoman military threat.

23
Courtyard of the Landhaus, the governmental palace built during the reign of Archduke Karl II, as seen from the Landeszeughaus.

A SURVEY OF EUROPEAN ARMS AND ARMOR

Walter J. Karcheski, Jr.

From the outset of armed combat, man has supplemented his own natural means of protection—skin and bone—with external defenses of various media. In Europe, the greatest technological and artistic advances in weaponry probably occurred between the mid thirteenth and seventeenth centuries. Combatants of all ranks found themselves facing an ever-changing arsenal of offensive weaponry, ranging from cold steel to fire-arms, which was pitted against the defensive craft and ingenuity of the armorer.

From about the time of the collapse of Rome to the middle of the thirteenth century, mail was the predominant form of metal body defense in Europe. Derived from the Old French word *maille* ("mesh"), mail is an interlocking metal armor of riveted and solid rings [figures 25, 26] worn over a suitably padded undergarment. It is now believed that mail originated among the pre-fifth-century B.C. Celtic peoples, and later spread eastward through Europe and the Middle East. During the Early and High Middle Ages, mail was fabricated as a long shirt, or hauberk, worn over the torso, limbs, and hands, and as a hood coif on the head and shoulders. Mail was expensive, however, and this restricted its use to the wealthy warrior and to those fortunate enough to obtain it in war.

Mail provided a reasonably reliable defense against the broadsword, the primary hand-held weapon of the period. This was a straight-bladed, double-edged weapon designed to deal hacking blows to an opponent. Although mail might withstand sword cuts, its loose openwork mesh provided only limited protection against either crushing arms like maces, war hammers, and axes, or piercing arms such as spears and crossbow projectiles. It was therefore necessary for the warrior to carry a leather-covered wooden shield to supplement the mail. Shield forms varied throughout the medieval period, but were generally either circular or, by the beginning of the fourteenth century, escutcheon-shaped, not unlike the underside of a flat iron.

24
Armor for an Infantry or Light Cavalry Officer, 1555–60 [checklist nos. 76.1–.2].

Armor made for infantry or lighter cavalry was intended to protect the head and torso, and only extended to above the knee. Mail sleeves and elbow-length gauntlets probably would have been worn with this armor.

25, 26
Mail Cape (with detail),
1500–1550 [checklist no. 45].

An interlocking network of
iron rings formed the fabric of
mail garments. Some soldiers
retained types of mail defenses
long after plate armor replaced
mail as the primary knightly
defense. The German
Landsknechte wore a mail cape,
sometimes called a "bishop's
mantle," well into the 16th
century.

On his head the medieval warrior wore either a conical helmet, a skullcap, or later, a large helm whose form was revised over the years until it rested on the shoulders. During the Crusades (1097–1291), European knights adopted their opponents' practice of wearing a loosely flowing outer garment, which became known as a surcoat.

Medieval battles such as the Battle of Hastings (1066) had demonstrated the value of heavy cavalry, but the furnishing, care, and maintenance of such horsemen was expensive and was therefore limited within the feudal system to knights, as they were called. The importance of the horse resulted in its protection with leather or mail trappers.

Despite its limitations, mail remained the primary bodily defense until about the middle of the thirteenth century. By that time, gradual experimentation with various media, including iron, led to the reintroduction of plate defenses, which had not been seen in such substantial numbers since the days of the Roman legions. Beginning with simple pieces on the limbs and larger ones to supplement the mail over the torso, plate armor eventually all but replaced the earlier defense. The trunk was protected by the coat-of-plates, which consisted of iron plates attached

27
Master of the Votive Tablet
of St. Lambrecht, *Votive Tablet
of St. Lambrecht* (detail), c. 1430
[checklist no. 43].

These soldiers' plate defenses
are partly covered by coat
armor that slightly predates the
period of this panel. The men
carry cut-and-thrust hand-and-
a-half swords. The lightly
furnished footsoldiers in the
foreground battle over a sack
of military booty.

to a poncho-like cover of leather or fabric, itself worn over layered
underdefenses of mail and soft armor. During the fourteenth century, this
mixed mail-and-plate defense gradually evolved into a more formfitting
shape, and those plates that protected the chest eventually formed a true
breastplate. This evolution also facilitated the development of the shock-
absorbing lance-rest, a device that was used into the seventeenth century.
In addition, the surcoat became tighter and shorter, in a form now called a
jupon, which was shaped like the contemporary civilian garment.

The equipment of the medieval common soldier varied, but consisted
of some form of padded or leather body defense, protection for the head,
and a weapon that might be a sword, a spear, or an agricultural implement
such as a bill hook, flail, or everyday ax or knife, all suitably modified for
more lethal use.

However, in 1326 a great technological breakthrough occurred with
the first recorded use of gunpowder weaponry. The earliest guns were
virtually immobile artillery pieces, but probably by the 1340s, and no
later than 1388, primitive yet portable handguns were in service. All of
these early handguns were crude, dangerous, and wildly inaccurate, but

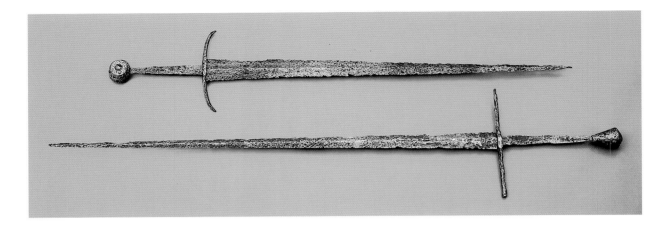

they could be physically and psychologically devastating. Nearly all seem to have been forged with a hook used as a recoil-absorbing device, giving use to the German name of *Hakenbüchse* (hook-gun), later corrupted to arquebus or harquebus. Such guns were ignited by manual application of a burning length of slow-match or a red-hot wire, and were held tightly to the body under the armpit, a technique that did little to enhance the shooter's accuracy.

28
Cut-and-Thrust Sword,
14th century [checklist no. 48].
Thrusting Sword, 15th century
[checklist no. 47].

Combination cut-and-thrust swords (above) and purely thrusting types (below) were weapons that could pierce solid defenses such as plate armor.

ARMOR AND WEAPONRY TO THE END OF THE FIFTEENTH CENTURY

By the end of the fourteenth century, therefore, well-articulated plate defenses had been created for the arms and legs, and the torso was also fully encased in plate. Except in Italy, where uncovered plate armor had already made its appearance, the body defenses remained cloth-covered to a great degree. As can be seen in the *Votive Tablet of St. Lambrecht* of c. 1430 [figure 27], the well-protected knight wore full arm and leg plate armor with fingered gauntlets on the hands, as well as laminated plate sabatons that were fashionably shaped so as to mirror the civilian footwear of the period. Mail supplemented the plate defenses in the form of hauberks, haubergeons, or neck defenses and hoods, as well as pieces worn to protect joints. Head defenses varied from mail-covered skullcaps to kettle-hats to basnets.

The weaponry of the horseman included the lance as the primary shock weapon, with sword and dagger as secondary sidearms. As plate armor became more common and effective, it became necessary to develop a weapon that could penetrate this defense. In order to puncture the plate, the older broadsword, designed almost exclusively for cutting, now assumed a second role as a thrusting arm. Blades became noticeably tapered, more rigid, and more lethal. In a move to enhance the force of a blow or thrust, the single-hand grip was lengthened. This created the "bastard" or "hand-and-a-half" sword, which was light enough to be used in one hand, but whose grip was long enough to accommodate several fingers of the other to facilitate more powerful attacks. Concurrently, another form of sword was used, beginning in the early 1400s, which was solely designed for the thrust. Sometimes called an *estoc* (from the French "to thrust"), this was a very stiff, acutely tapered weapon of lozenge cross section. A mounted combatant could thus carry both forms of sword—a "bastard" cut-and-thrust sword worn on the left hip and a thrusting form (occasionally wielded in a lance-like manner at the armpit for more control and piercing force) at the saddle [figure 28]. A dagger was also often worn on the swordbelt. A sword poised to deliver a thrust also facilitated parrying, thus a new aspect of swordplay came into being.

29
Halberd, 1500–1525 [checklist no. 100]; Pankraz Taller, Halberd, 1582–86 [checklist no. 107]; Peter Schreckeisen, Glaive, c. 1575 [checklist no. 116]; Pike, 1575–1600 [checklist no. 140].

The most rudimentary hafted weapons, commonly called polearms, evolved from agricultural tools during the late medieval period. Eventually, specialized infantrymen used new forms that were developed as military weapons.

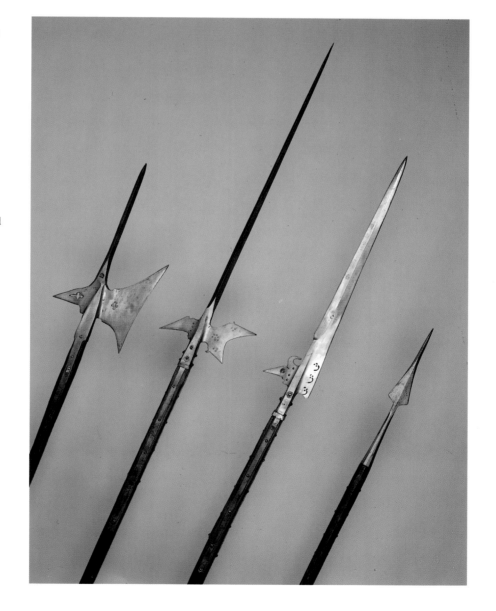

Footsoldiers also experienced changes in their arsenal. During the late thirteenth century, a combination arm called a halberd was developed. It united an ax, a spear, and a hook-like fluke in one weapon [figure 29]. The spear-like long pike, neglected since the days of ancient Greece, was revived at the end of the fourteenth century. For the most part, however, infantry remained very much a secondary force.

Arms developed for purely ceremonial purposes seem to have first appeared during the fourteenth century with the bearing or ceremonial sword [figure 30]. Such swords could be gifts from the pope to defenders of the faith, or from the emperor to a particularly deserving subject. In any event, these swords were never intended as war weapons. Many are grossly oversized or ornately decorated. All serve as the physical embodiment of the prowess and power of the state and of the individual who dispensed that power.

The sporting combats called jousts and tournaments also figure strongly in the evolution of arms and armor. From the eleventh to the thirteenth centuries, the equipment of real war was used, almost without provision for additional protection or personal restraint. Consequently, many participants were maimed or killed. Periodic bans by church and state notwithstanding, the games persisted, and finally, by the mid thirteenth century, specially designed weapons such as the blunted lance were introduced. At the same time, two distinct games were defined—the "joust of peace," employing safety equipment and only intended to unseat one's opponent and shatter his lances, and the "joust of war," where the use of combat equipment often resulted in injury or death. Although men did not strive to injure or kill their opponents, they still were attracted to the ever-present element of danger, which appealed to their courage and machismo.

By the fifteenth century, the transition from mail to full, uncovered plate armor was complete. The century was still to see great advances in the artistic and functional refinement of armor and arms. To students, this period is the apogee of the armorer's craft, combining aesthetic and functional purity. Unfortunately, only about one dozen complete or near-complete, homogeneous, high-quality armors of the period are known to survive, so our knowledge is shaped largely by the iconography of armor or by individual elements alone. Plate armor mirrored civilian costume in the form of its components, so long as this fashion-consciousness did not interfere with the function of the pieces. For example, when plate foot defenses, or sabatons, were worn during the fifteenth century (largely outside of Italy, where mail was generally preferred), they were made in

32

30
Ceremonial Sword, c. 1600 [checklist no. 209].

This gilt sword is from a class of edged weapons that were often elaborately designed and decorated. These weapons were purely ceremonial, borne during parades and important public events to symbolize an individual's office and power.

the long, tapered, so-called Gothic style. At this time armor was also made for specific battlefield or sporting functions. For example, lighter cavalry or infantry wore breastplates without a lance-rest, as the type of lance used, or the fact that none was carried, made it unnecessary. In addition, armor for the horse also reached its peak in the fifteenth century. Until the second half of the sixteenth century, horse armor would be a part of the finest armor sets, often created to match that of the rider [figure 33].

The armor of the fifteenth century, the so-called Gothic fashion, appeared in variations of the Italian and German styles, with those produced at Innsbruck being a blend of the two. The Italianate form was smooth, rounded, and robust, sometimes even appearing bulky. The German style, on the other hand, was sharper, more angular, and form-fitting, with arched lines reminiscent of Gothic architecture. Breast and backplates were flexible and supple, constructed of multiple plates working on rivets and internal leathers. The earlier basnet helmet gradually went out of style, and was replaced by the Italian barbut, the close-fitting visored armet, or the sallet. Graceful, with a rounded skull and sweeping tail, the sallet is perhaps the headpiece most readily associated with Gothic armor. As it protected only the upper part of the face and head, it was generally supplemented by a bevor for the lower face and throat [figures 31, 32]. By the early sixteenth century, the throat was protected by the articulated collar, or gorget, which enclosed the neck and defended the vital link between helmet and cuirass.

Special armor was also made for service on foot and for general use by infantry. Infantrymen tended to disdain expensive or unnecessary elements, and favored light armor that did not restrict their agility. Footsoldiers preferred the brigandine, a lighter descendant of the coat-of-plates. Since infantry seldom used gauntlets, the sword essentially became the defense for the hand, with bars and plates being added to the hilt. This transition set the groundwork for ever more elaborate systems of hilts. Firearms also grew in importance for the infantry, becoming the chief missile weapon during the second half of the fifteenth century. This was due in large part to the introduction of the matchlock, a mechanical ignition system that relieved the gunner of the chore of manually applying the slow-match while aiming at the target. This cheap, simple, and reliable gunlock endured, with only minor changes, until the end of the seventeenth century. Rifling was also apparently developed toward the end of the fifteenth century, although most weapons remained smoothbore.

34

31, 32
Workshop in the town of
Villach in Carinthia, *St. George*
(with detail), c. 1520 [checklist
no. 62].

St. George wears the transitional armor of the early
Maximilian period that, while
fashionably rounded, retains
such Gothic details as the
rippled ribs on the breastplate,
thighs, and arms, and the use
of the sallet helmet with bevor.

33 ▶
School of Konrad Seusenhofer,
Horse Armor, 1505–10; Saddle
and Stirrups, 1530–1540
[checklist nos. 57.1–.2].

A knight's effectiveness
depended greatly on his horse.
The horse could be outfitted
with armor to varying degrees,
depending on its combat or
sporting role. The most
complete ensemble of horse
armor was the full bard; this
one is contemporary with the
riders' armors of the Mariazell
altarpiece [figure 11] and with
the "Maximilian" armor by
Hans Maystetter [figure 12].

Edged weapons and hafted arms continued to play an important role on the battlefield. Hand-and-a-half swords were widely used, and an even larger weapon, the two-handed sword, was employed by infantry in great numbers [figures 40, 42, 43]. The two-handed sword had already been developed before the middle of the fourteenth century. As a specialist weapon of veteran troops, it disrupted other infantry formations and cut through the staffs of pikes and other hafted arms. The saber also became more popular with light horsemen, particularly the cavalry of eastern Europe [figures 34, 36].

SPORTING COMBAT

Jousts and tournaments peaked at the end of the fifteenth to the first half of the sixteenth centuries [figure 37]. By this time they were sports conducted for their own sake, with no pretense of being preparatory training for real war. The sporting equipment was often specially made for the endlessly varied games. More safety features were introduced, such as the tilt from Italy. This was a wall-like barrier that separated the mounted combatants, prevented head-on collisions of the horses, and reduced the impact of a lance to a glancing blow delivered in passing. Complete head-to-toe armor was necessary, however, for one could easily crush a leg between tilt and horse. Since the participants' left sides were those most exposed to the lance, the armor for that side was thicker and more fully reinforced with add-on plates [figure 38]. By the reign of Emperor Maximilian I (reigned 1493–1519), there were at least eleven different forms of mounted jousts and tournaments in German lands, not to mention ceremonial combats on foot. The latter were an outgrowth of earlier man-to-man combat, but by the middle of the fifteenth century, they had been codified and confined within a corral-like area called the

34
Saber with Scabbard,
1550–1600 [checklist no. 66].

The eastern European light cavalry was greatly influenced by its Ottoman counterpart. Following their enemies' example, German soldiers lightly armed themselves with lances and cutting sabers.

35

Shield for a Hussar, early 16th century [checklist no. 65].

This practical shield style was widespread throughout east-central Europe. It curved to the body and the upper edge swept up and out, protecting the wearer without obscuring his vision. The low notch in the upper edge supported the hussar's lance.

36

Danube School, Master of the Brucker Panel of St. Martin, Panel from the *Legend of St. Sigismund*, c. 1520 [checklist no. 64].

This panel is from an altarpiece that illustrates eight scenes from the life of St. Sigismund, a 6th-century Burgundian king who was converted to Christianity. This detail of the Frankish invasion of Burgundy illustrates the equipment of the European light horseman. In addition to saber and shield, each horseman carries a lance with pennon. The upper parts of the horses' hindquarters are protected by some form of light crupper. The atmospheric landscape, the expressive strength, and the brilliant colors are typical of paintings of the Danube School.

lists. Various weapons, from swords to pikes and from halberds to throwing axes, were employed. Quite understandably, tempers flared readily, requiring armored referees who entered the lists and separated the combatants. Like the mounted sporting combats, specialized armor and arms were employed for the sake of safety.

THE PRODUCTION OF ARMS

During the fifteenth century, the manufacture and provision of military equipment had become a thriving industry in much of Europe. German cities such as Passau and, later, Solingen became renowned for their blades [figure 40]. Many of the swords used in and around Graz came from local workshops in Weiz and Judenberg, while others were fitted with blades from Passau. Styrian harquebuses and halberds were turned out in large numbers. Among foreign armorers, Milan was the largest center of armor production at the time. Her prodigious armorers sent their wares far and wide, and were readily copied. By the end of the fifteenth century, German centers had made inroads into this Italian near-monopoly, and during the next century they would largely control the industry. As evidenced by the Landeszeughaus collection, the city of Nuremberg was one of the greatest centers of production in terms of both quantity and quality. The economic importance of arms production to the city had been recognized before the end of the fourteenth century.

37
The Great Tournament in Vienna,
c. 1570 [checklist no. 94].

Tournaments were popular spectacles held in royal or public places. This picture illustrates the Austrian nobility who participated in one of the ceremonial combats held in Vienna in 1560, honoring the visit of Duke Albrecht V of Bavaria.

38
Armor for the Joust over the Tilt, in the Italian Manner *(Plankengestech nach Italienischer Art)*, 1570–1580 [checklist no. 97].

This example shows the asymmetry of jousting armor. In the *Plankengestech* course, the participants rode along a wall-like tilt, with their left sides facing. A combatant could only make an oblique blow directed against an opponent's left side; consequently, armor on that side was thicker and more strongly reinforced. In the German manner of *Plankengestech,* a steel, shield-like tilting-target was fixed to the armor in place of the formfitting grandguard of the Italian style.

39 ▶▶
Half Armors for Light Cavalry, comprised of burgonet, cuirass, and almain collar, 1560–1570.

Everyday ammunitions-quality armor was generally plain and uncomplicated. These half armors were probably made for pistoleers or harquebusiers and were blackened, a technique that simplified production and reduced maintenance.

42

40
Two-handed sword, made in
southern Germany, c. 1600
[checklist no. 82].

Rigid controls and standards were set to ensure quality. Most of the items made were what are known as "ammunition" grade—in effect, government-issue material—and a portion of this production went directly to the local garrison [figure 39]. As in other centers, the arms industry in Nuremberg was very specialized. Cutlers, for example, made knives, civilian swords, and decorative hilts; swordsmiths made only the blades themselves. Armorers were subdivided into mail and plate armor makers, and shield makers belonged to a branch of the painters' trade.

The standards set for armorers were very high indeed. In order to be a master, a journeyman had to produce a quality product for each type of component he wished to make. To be designated a complete master, separate examples of helmet, cuirass, arm and leg defenses, and gauntlets had to be reviewed by five designated master inspectors. After this critique, the applicant's status and mark were duly registered in a double set of books. Less-demanding products were also permitted, but these received a distinguishing punch. Only qualified masters who were licensed to sell their own products could do so.

The reputation Nuremberg gained was due not only to its craftsmen's skills, but also to the quality of its raw materials. The best iron ore came from the regions around Innsbruck and, interestingly, from Styria. Using local charcoal and water power, a steely iron was refined and beaten into sheets that were then provided to the shops. When building a custom armor, the armorer secured either the measurements, a sample garment, or wax models of the limbs of the client. Most of the ammunition-grade armor was probably prepared using templates in small, medium, or large sizes. Cut to rough outlines, the plates were heated and first shaped by hammermen. So formed, the pieces were then turned over to the master, his two journeymen, four apprentices, and at times, other assistants. Throughout the manufacturing process the pieces were inspected and the results noted. Armor components were test-fitted and evaluated before and after their final finish. Those components that were to be "proof," or bullet-resistant, for example, were fired at from a set distance, using the most appropriate type of firearm. The resulting dent, which often appears on such armor, is called a proof mark. Those not of proof were called "light" or "good and sufficient." Once armor was given its final finish and fitted with its various buckles, hinges, straps, and linings, the master then applied his mark. If the city's final examiners approved, they also stamped Nuremberg's half-eagle coat of arms, the *Beschau,* or view-mark, upon it [figure 41].

41
Half Armor for Infantry (detail), c. 1578.

This detail shows the view-mark applied by the city of Nuremberg to weapons and armors made there.

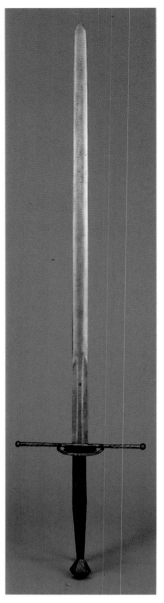

44

THE SIXTEENTH CENTURY

In the development of arms and armor during the sixteenth century, the first two decades belong to Emperor Maximilian I. Maximilian was a great patron of arms, as evidenced in his thinly anonymous autobiography *Weisskunig* and the tournament codex *Freydal*. He also recognized the importance of well-stocked regional arsenals (*Zeughäuser*), which he furnished with armor and arms.

In 1499 Maximilian ended his own wars with the Swiss Confederation and became embroiled in the Italian Wars against France. Although he considered himself "the last knight," Maximilian fully appreciated the value of professional, dedicated infantry, and created his own force, calling them *Landsknechte*. In imitation of the Swiss, who were

42
Landsknecht Hans von Lonispergh, 1540 [checklist no. 78].

Von Lonispergh carries his two-handed sword just as a rifle is carried today.

43
Two-handed Sword, 1530–1540 [checklist no. 75].

Despite its great size, the infantry two-handed sword weighed an average of only eight to ten pounds. Mastering these swords required specialized training and was an enviable accomplishment.

44, 45, 46
Field Armor of the
"Maximilian" form (with
details), c. 1520 [checklist
no. 58].

This style of armor, named for
Emperor Maximilian, featured
rounded surfaces, frequent
fluted decoration, "mitten"
gauntlets, and broad-toed
sabatons. Seven of the eight
Maximilian armors in the
Landeszeughaus were recorded
in an inventory of 1557.

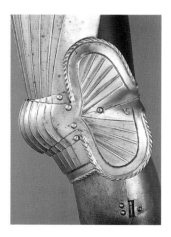

employed by his French opponents, Maximilian's infantry men were mercenaries. *Landsknechte* were unarmored or very lightly armored. Men in the front ranks wore a breastplate with tassets, a light helmet, and perhaps a mail cape protecting the neck and shoulders [figure 42]. They carried halberds, two-handed swords, harquebuses, and, most often, pikes. Virtually all carried a short sword for close combat. Possibly the most distinctive feature of these troops was their "puffed and slashed" garment fashion, sometimes carried to outrageous extremes [figure 96].

For about the first forty years of the sixteenth century, horsemen continued to be comprised of light and heavy cavalry. In the eastern regions, light cavalry or *Stradiots* were still influenced by their Turkish equivalents, lightly protected by shield [figure 36], hat or light helmet, saber, lance, and thrusting sword. The heavy cavalry throughout Europe remained the heavily armored knight or man-at-arms with lance and sword. In German lands, the armors worn by such forces reflected another stylistic change, the form that we now call "Maximilian" armor, in honor of the emperor. This type represents the synthesis of the German Gothic angularity with the rounded plastic quality of the Italian style. In its earliest examples it was rounded and sometimes extremely plain, with decoration limited to shell-like ripples on the breastplate and other curved surfaces [figures 31, 74]. As the style evolved during the first quarter of the century, flutes were introduced, first in groups, and later spread evenly over the surface [figures 44, 45, 46]. This overall fluting was the metal equivalent of the civilian doublet cinched by a waistbelt. In addition, this corrugation made the plate more rigid without additional thickness. This fashion was seldom seen outside of Germany, and no doubt in part due to the additional work and resulting expense inherent in its manu-facture, the style declined after 1525 and was passé by about 1540.

As before, armor styles were closely related to trends in civilian costume. "Maximilian" armors had globose breastplates and the broad-toed shoe form of the time. As the century progressed, styles changed according to the prevailing trends and the evolving needs of the armor. By the beginning of the fourth decade, the rounded breastplate was super-seded by a slimmer one with a medial ridge [figure 85]. As years passed, there was a tendency for this ridge to curve outward and down toward the waistline [figure 24], until by the 1580s the fully dipped "peascod" (from peapod) shape of breastplate was in vogue.

A medium cavalry class of horsemen was created during the sixteenth century. These men wore three-quarter armor that reached to just below the knees and often had a lance-rest on the breastplate. Half armor was

47
Sebastian Schmid, Half Armor
for Service on Foot (detail),
c. 1555 [checklist no. 74].

This detail illustrates the
blackened, rough surface of the
armor plate, and the brightly
polished, raised plain band
and flame-like foliate edging.
"Black-and-white" armor is
named for this alternately dark
and bright treatment.

also worn by horsemen as well as some infantry officers. These armors
were often heat-treated or painted to reduce maintenance and inhibit
corrosion. Many were partly blackened, with contrasting brightly
polished areas, raised or recessed, as part of the forging process [figure
47]. Just before the middle of the sixteenth century, pistoleer cavalry
came into being. These troops, sometimes called *Schwarze Reiter* ("Black
Riders") after the darkened armors they wore, carried sword, estoc,
dagger, and lance, or a brace of pistols. Soon these troops relied almost
exclusively on their firepower [figure 49]. Unlike the matchlock with its
smoldering slow-match, the wheel-locks they used had spark-producing
ignition systems. A spring-tensioned wheel was cocked or spanned using
a special key called a spanner. When the trigger was pulled, the wheel
spun from the sudden release of tension, rotated against a piece of iron
pyrite clamped in the jaws of the cock, thus producing sparks, much like

a cigarette lighter. These sparks fell into a small pan containing priming powder poured from a special flask. When ignited, the powder in turn set off the main charge. While inherently safer than the matchlock, wheel-lock ignitions were not without their problems. Since they were rather complex, they required careful manufacture that meant they were more expensive and required more maintenance. Although they could be loaded and spanned in advance, this could not be done too far ahead, as the spring could weaken and lose the stored tension needed to turn the wheel. In addition, the very advantage of advance arming meant, ironically, that there was a real danger of accidental discharge. These limitations aside, the wheel-lock afforded a comparatively safe, reliable ignition system that was an alternative to the matchlock, and that made smaller firearms a reality. From the second half of the sixteenth century on, most horsemen, even lancers, carried at least one pistol or other

49
Clockwise from top:
Wheel-lock Pistol for a
Horseman, 1575–1600
[checklist no. 162]; Spanner,
1575–1600 [checklist no. 165];
Leather Holster, 1575–1600
[checklist no. 167]; Cartridge
Box, 1590–1600 [checklist no.
164]; and Priming Flask,
1575–1600 [checklist no. 163].

The invention of the wheel-lock ignition about 1500 made possible small firearms that could be fired with one hand. In addition to the pistol and leather holster, the horseman had a spanner to wind the lock and gauge the bullets, a cartridge box, and a round priming flask.

Wheel-lock gun, barrel dated
1527, stock decoration
1570–1580 [checklist no. 87].

50
Sporting Crossbow with
Winder and Bolt, second half
of the 16th century [checklist
nos. 224.1–.3].

The crossbow remained
popular for target shooting and
hunting long after the mid 16th
century, when firearms made
it obsolete for war. Its advan-
tages as a sporting weapon
were clear: it was clean and
quiet, and it fired reusable
projectiles, called bolts or
quarrels. The Habsburg double
eagle on the stock of this bow
suggests a connection with the
imperial house.

firearm. In fact, because of their ability to use firearms, cavalry remained viable even with the gradual demise of the lance. Earlier forms of missile weapons such as longbows and crossbows gradually faded from the battlefield during the century, but remained popular as hunting or sport-ing arms [figure 50].

The changing requirements of infantry and the lighter cavalry resulted in the burgonet helmet, which could be worn open or supple-mented by a facial defense called a falling-buffe [figure 87], whose plates could be raised or lowered at will. Simple skullcap-like sallets remained popular with many infantrymen until about the middle of the sixteenth century. In central and western Europe, officers of infantry, other ranks, and some horsemen used the open morion helmet [figure 76] with tall comb and downturned brim. The cabasset and closely related comb-cap evolved from the Spanish *capacete*. It had an almond-shaped skull with a narrow, flat brim, making it popular with many firearm-equipped infantry and pikemen [figures 16, 17]. The most-used helmet among the heavy cavalry was the close helmet. Like the earlier armet, this totally enclosed the head, but all of its elements worked on a common set of mounts at the temples. The introduction of a two-piece visor assembly meant that a part could still cover most of the face while the upper portion could be raised for better vision and ventilation [figure 73].

49

SPECIAL ARMOR

By at least the fourteenth century, arms and armor had been made for the sons of important individuals who aspired to the knightly class. Such items were not intended as war equipment, but mirrored faithfully the full-sized items used by their fathers [figure 51]. Also used in greater numbers were armors made for the retinue and bodyguards of important officials and nobility, such as the *Trabants* (subordinate commanders) of Georg Khevenhüller zu Aichelberg, Baron of Landskron and Weinberg [figures 52, 53].

High-quality armor for the field was made for important clients such as Archduke Karl II of Inner Austria. The combat armor made by Conrad Richter that he wore during his 1566 campaign against the Turkish invaders is preserved in the Landeszeughaus [figure 54]. The close helmet of this armor has a provision for a reinforcing plate on the visor assembly, indicating that it was designed to be modified for various purposes and suggesting that it was part of a small garniture.

The garniture was probably the most remarkable achievement of the armorer's art. Simply put, a garniture was a grouping of various reinforcing pieces and interchangeable elements for a field armor, permitting different combinations for specific functions. While each component served its own function, all the pieces needed to harmonize in a physical and decorative sense. The small garniture's elements enabled its use as a full armor, a three-quarter length horseman's armor, a half armor for dismounted use, and a foot-tourney armor for the sporting combat at the waist-height barriers. A light armor for the horse was also included. Closely related to the small garniture was the double armor, a field armor provided with only those pieces needed for certain tournament and jousting events. The great garniture was the most complex and the most versatile set of armor, sometimes comprising nearly one hundred major elements. Understandably, garnitures are usually only partially preserved. The Landeszeughaus retains about two dozen pieces from a great garniture built for Kaspar, baron of Völs-Schenkenberg, for a royal tournament held at Vienna in 1560 [figure 55]. Like Karl II, Völs-Schenkenberg also campaigned against the Turks in 1564–66, and may have worn the field armor portions of the set at that time.

Although knightly jousts, tournaments, and foot combats were fashionable through the first half of the sixteenth century, following the gruesome death of the French monarch Henry II during a joust in 1559, they entered into an irreversible decline. Mounted jousts were replaced

51
Armor for an Adult and a Youth. From left to right: Sebastian Schmid, Half Armor for Service on Foot, c. 1555 [checklist no. 74]; Wolfgang Prenner the Younger, Armor for a Youth, c. 1540 [checklist no. 73].

Diminutive armor and weapons were fabricated for the sons of the nobility, so that young men in training for the knighthood could familiarize themselves with the equipment. As the shift toward massed-infantry tactics signaled a decline in the knight's role, training these youths became less necessary. As a result, arms and armor for the young increasingly became symbols of social status.

52, 53
Black-and-White Three-quarter
Armor for an Officer of
Bodyguards (with detail),
c. 1575 [checklist no. 123].

This and a similar armor
entered the Landeszeughaus
from the armory of the
Khevenhüller family at Burg
Hochosterwitz. Both armors
have etched medallions framing
the crucified Christ and a
kneeling knight. This armor
has the additional motif of oak
leaves surmounted by a "K."
The acorn (*Eichel* in German)
represents Aichelberg, the seat
of the Khevenhüller family. A
number of armors and weapons
decorated with this device
remain at Hochosterwitz.

54

Conrad Richter, Field Armor of Archduke Karl II of Inner Austria, c. 1565 [checklist no. 69].

Elegant lines distinguish this armor built by Conrad Richter of Augsburg, probably for Karl's 1566 campaign against the Ottomans. Note the folding, shock-absorbing lance-rest and the cutaway pauldron, enabling the lance to be firmly set or "couched" under the arm when used. This armor appears on Karl's marble effigy in the monastery at Seckau in Austria.

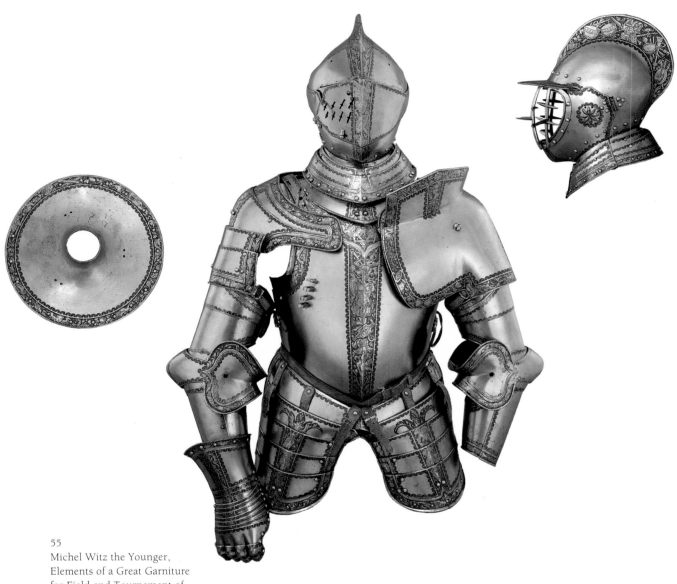

55
Michel Witz the Younger,
Elements of a Great Garniture
for Field and Tournament of
Kaspar Baron Völs-Schenkenberg,
1560 [checklist nos. 96.1–.3].

The components above are
preserved from the heavy full
armor for combat assembled for
the *Freiturnier* (a mounted
sporting combat between teams
wearing reinforced field armors)
with the vamplate (handguard)
of the lance. The complete
armor is shown diagramatically.

Above is a burgonet with
barred, spiked visor, from
a light armor for the field
(*Feldküriss*). The diagram
shows those components
that would have been worn
with the breastplate, tassets,
and gauntlets from the heavy
full armor, together with mail
sleeves.

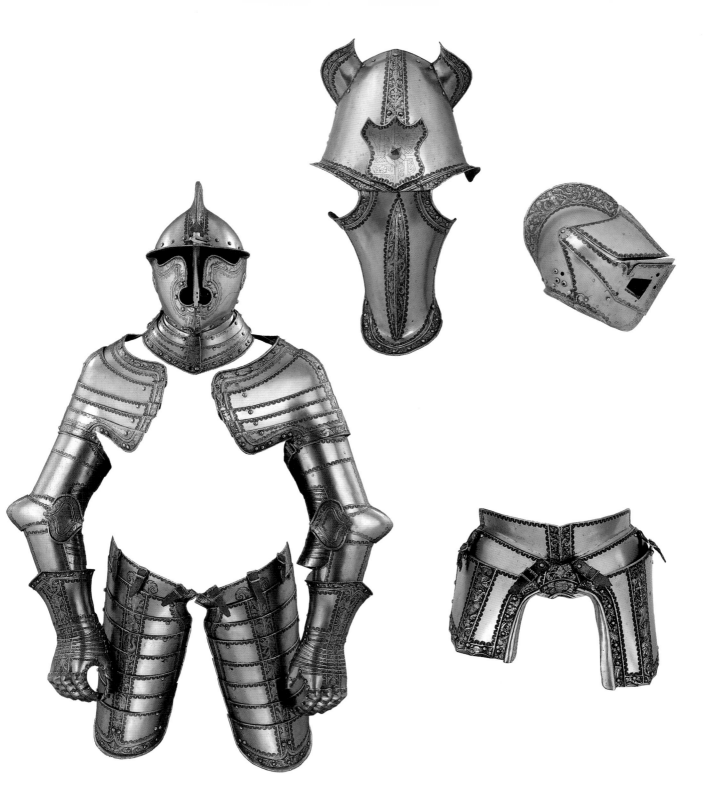

 The preserved elements from the half armor for mounted service without lance, known as *Harnasch,* are shown above with a full shaffron for the horse. The pauldrons may be from a set for the friendly sporting combats on foot, known as *Fussturnier.*

 Above are the close helmet and waistlame with tassets from the jousting armor for the *Plankengestech.* The iron shield, known as a tilting-target, is in the collection of the Hermitage, St. Petersburg. The diagramed components would have been worn over the breastplate, tassets, arms, and legs from the heavy full armor.

by the carousel, an elaborate equestrian ballet that was more a show of horsemanship than a demonstration of martial prowess. An old event, the quintain, also acquired new popularity. Here a lancer attempted to deliver a clean thrust to a pivoted demi-figure. If executed poorly, the figure spun around, striking the horseman with an embarrassing blow. Some of these figures were modeled on that age-old enemy, the Turk [figure 56].

As the sixteenth century progressed, combatants wore fewer pieces of armor, despite first-rate workmanship and the mechanical splendor of the garniture [figures 59, 60]. Consistently improved firearms meant that thicker pieces of plate were required, which concentrated protection where it was needed most. The best armors continued to be tested exhaustively, but such armor of proof was heavy and cumbersome.

The effect of firearms was not ignored but led to revised tactics. Within their inherent technical limits, firearms were perfected. The

56

56
The Turk of Saurau Palace, c. 1600 [checklist no. 56].

Figures of militant Turks such as this were popular opponents in the quintain course.

heavier musket [figures 62, 63] replaced the harquebus as the chief military longarm during the 1580s. Having an effective range of some two hundred yards, muskets fired a lead ball that could penetrate all but the best armor at sixty to seventy yards. Loading and firing such weapons, however, was laboriously slow, for a musketeer could at best get off one to two shots per minute. In an attempt to overcome this, some weapons were made with multiple barrels, or could fire superimposed charges from one barrel [figures 57, 58].

Wheel-lock guns [figure 61] were appropriate for use on horseback by mounted harquebusiers, a type of horseman armed with a heavy carbine. As in other European countries, at this time the term harquebus denoted a moderately sized long arm used by footsoldiers and cavalry alike. The latter troops, known in German lands as *Arkebusier-Reiter,* were recorded as early as 1502, and by mid century were equipped with harquebus, open helmet, almain collar, cuirass or breastplate, and sword. In sixteenth-century Styria they were widely used in operations along the highly volatile borders. They were largely Hungarian and Croatian troops, as were the light cavalry generically known as hussars, who were similarly employed. Hussars were armed in the eastern fashion. They wore *Zischägge* helmet, a laminated or a waistcoat cuirass, and a mail shirt and they might carry a combination of lance, saber, estoc, mace, and a pistol [figure 64].

57, 58
Master "IP" (barrelmaker) and Master "HM" (stockmaker), Double-barreled, Double Wheel-lock Pistol, c. 1580 [checklist no. 216].

Two-Shot Superimposed-charge Gun with Double Wheel-lock, c. 1600 [checklist no. 88].

There were many attempts made during the 16th and 17th centuries to increase the rate of fire in both longarms and pistols. Multi-barreled pistols were made from the 1530s to the 19th century, when they were superseded by revolving arms.

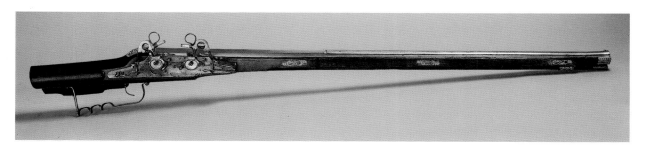

58

59

Archduke Ferdinand of Inner Austria, 1600–1610 [checklist no. 149].

In this painting, Ferdinand wears a darkened half armor with gilded borders, of the form used for dismounted combat or perhaps for the sporting combats with sword and pike at the barriers. Major components of armor such as pauldrons and tassets were fabric-lined to avoid metal rubbing on metal, and the scalloped edges, called pickadils, decorated the armor.

60 ▶

Attributed to Heinrich De Veerle, *Portrait of Ruprecht von Eggenberg,* c. 1675–80 [checklist no. 192].

Although painted some sixty-five years after Ruprecht's death, this portrait quite accurately depicts portions of an Augsburg armor he may have worn during his service with the Spanish imperial army. The style of this armor strongly suggests that it was made by Anton Peffenhauser, an Augsburg armorer and a favorite of the imperial house during the reign of Charles V. Ruprecht had a distinguished military career that included the defeat of the Ottoman army at the Battle of Sissek.

60

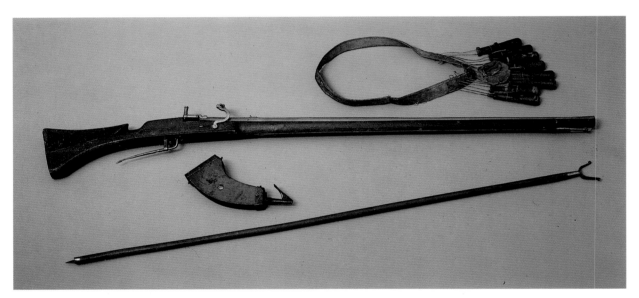

Styrians were acutely aware of the ever-present Ottoman threat and the need for adequate stocks of military equipment. From the early sixteenth century, they were well-served with a variety of artillery, and from about 1566 detachments of wheel-lock riflemen supplemented large bodies of heavily armored pikemen and the musketeers. In 1575 government ordinances dictated the extensive rearming of Styria. Styria placed orders with Nuremberg in 1577 that were filled over the following two years. Nuremberg produced impressive quantities of material, including 4,532 marksmen's helmets, 389 half-armors for pikemen, 206 light cavalry armors, more than 600 combination match and wheel-lock guns, plus 122 pairs of pistols and accessories. About a decade later, Graz placed orders with Nuremberg's rival, Augsburg, and additional guns, swords, and halberds were made locally.

62
From top: Bandoleer, 17th century [checklist no. 237]; Matchlock Musket, 1600–1620 [checklist no. 235]; Powder Flask, 1600–1650 [checklist no. 239]; and Musket Rest, 1600–1650 [checklist no. 236].

The matchlock remained the most common form of gunlock on European infantry longarms until the end of the 17th century. The musket was more accurate and had a greater range than the harquebus, but its long barrel often required a forked rest. The bandoleer held premeasured charges.

From top: Wheel-lock Musket, c. 1600 [checklist no. 222]; Combined Match- and Wheel-lock Musket, c. 1600 [checklist no. 220]; and Nikolaus Karpf, Wheel-lock Harquebus, c. 1590–1600 [checklist no. 223].

These firearms were probably made for use by a city or provincial guard unit. The shorter wheel-lock harquebus was perhaps carried by a mounted guard (*Trabant*) or a form of light horseman known as an *Arkebusier-Reiter*. The two longer muskets also have the older, reliable matchlock, used in the event of the wheel-lock's failure.

63
Jacob de Gheyn,
Waffenhandlung von den Roren,
(detail) [checklist no. 234].

61

EARLY MODERN WARFARE— THE SEVENTEENTH CENTURY

With the exception of our own era, the first half of the seventeenth century was probably the most destructive period in European military history. In describing this situation, one historian has suggested that, lacking a full stock of supplies, the soldiers were like giant maggots digging for provisions. When they disbanded at the end of a season of campaigning to seek winter quarters, the soldiers became little better than armed hoodlums, terrorizing friend and foe alike. The forces were largely infantry with supporting cavalry and artillery components. Infantry "squares" of the time were massive, slothlike tactical formations of more than twenty-five hundred pikemen and musketeers in nearly equal

64

Jost Amman and Tobias
Stimmer, *Dess Neuwen
Kunstbuchs . . .*, 1570–1580
[checklist no. 176].

This plate shows the hussar's
armor with *Zischägge* and
cuirass. This soldier is equipped in the manner of hussar
cavalry; however, he wears full
plate arm defenses in place of
the mail sleeves of the Styrian
hussars.

65 ▶

Interior View of the
Landeszeughaus Graz, with
Hans Prenner, Infantry Half
Armors and Burgonets,
1615–1631.

From the beginning of the
17th century, armorers in Graz
began to produce much of the
city's armor. The armorer
Hans Prenner made more than
one thousand armors like this
over a sixteen-year period.
These austere, hammer-rough
armors were intended for
pikemen and other heavy
infantry.

proportions. Pikemen continued to wear half armors, and those who felt particularly exposed might also carry a bulletproof rondache shield. Other infantrymen carried the few hafted arms still in use, largely halberds, which by this date had degenerated into little more than long spikes with feeble axheads. Many others became purely decorative arms carried by guards [figure 67]. As early as the 1630s, the pike's importance began to wane. Before the end of the century, the bayonet effectively made each musketeer his own pikeman, and in the eighteenth century, the pike slipped into obscurity.

Footsoldiers with firearms generally did not wear armor except, perhaps, for the occasional light helmet or a skullcap worn beneath the large felt hats of the period. Due to their simplicity and economy, match-lock ignitions continued to be used on infantry long arms, while after the 1670s the flintlock quickly replaced the wheel-lock. However, the wheel-lock remained popular on sporting guns [figure 68], and in German lands, it served into the early nineteenth century.

Contrafactur Graf Nicklas von Serin.

Ich Keiserliche Mayestat   Da ich dem Türcken wider Stan   Doch bald sein handt abzuge Gott
Zu General gesetzet hat   Mit manchen trew Redlichen Man   Da wurden wir geschlagen Todt
Zu der befestigung Sigette   So lang vns Gott sein hilff hat than Vnd kam Siget in angst vnd not.

66

Count Niklas Zrinyi, c. 1566
[checklist no. 77.2].

In 1566 the Ottoman sultan
Süleyman the Magnificent lay
siege to one of the Hungarian
fortresses, Szigetvár, held by
the forces of Count Niklas
Zrinyi. After his valiant efforts
to defend the fortress failed,
Zrinyi ordered its destruction
and died with his troops in a
final, desperate attack. In this
woodcut, Zrinyi wears half
armor and eastern European-
influenced costume.

67

Ceremonial Partisan for the
Guard of Hans Franz von
Stainach, 1628 [checklist
no. 215].

As they became less important
for combat, exquisitely decorated staff weapons assumed a
greater role as ceremonial arms
for bodyguards.

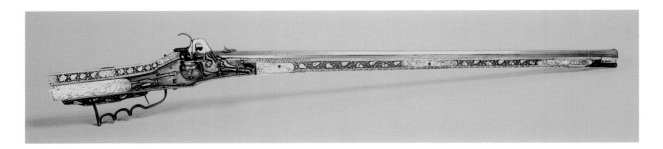

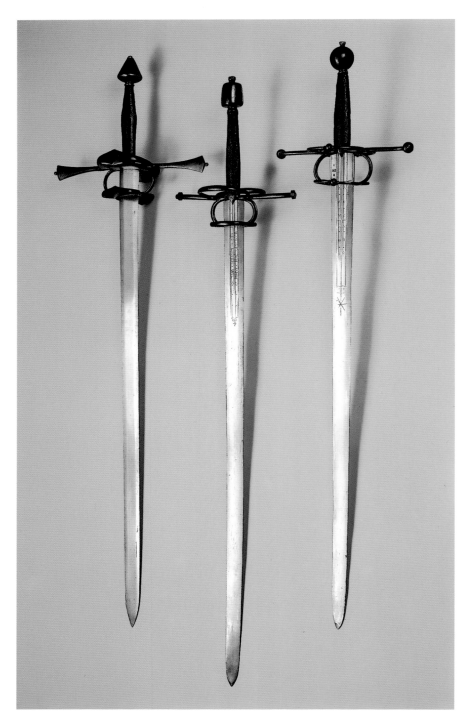

68
Master "ND," Wheel-lock Hunting Rifle, c. 1580 [checklist no. 226].

Hunting arms often represented the highest form of the gunmaker's art, as they were usually made for wealthy clients who could afford the best technology and craftsmanship. This stock has a "German" butt, designed to be pressed tightly to the cheek and gripped firmly in the recesses of the trigger guard. This gun has both set and hair triggers, permitting advance arming. Once engaged, only the slightest touch on the hair trigger would discharge the rifle, enabling the sportsman to keep his sights on the target.

69
Hand-and-a-half Sword, 16th century [checklist no. 85]; Sword, 1580–1620 [checklist no. 282]; Sword, 1580–1620 [checklist no. 280].

The two swords on the right are combination cut-and-thrust weapons, probably carried by cuirassiers during the opening years of the Thirty Years' War.

70
Philips Wouwerman, *Soldiers in Baggage Train,* c. 1650 [checklist no. 233].

This work, by one of the best 17th-century horse painters, clearly illustrates contemporary cavalry garb. The central horsemen wear thick, long-paneled "buff" leather coats, often stout enough to turn a sword blow. In addition, both men have iron cuirasses to defend against gunshot. The red waist sash denotes affiliation with the Habsburg Empire's forces.

THE DECLINE OF ARMOR

By the 1620s, cavalry had all but abandoned the lance. It retained some popularity among eastern European horsemen, notably the hussars in Austria and Poland, who retained the weapon into the 1680s. The lance was never popular in the forested, mountainous regions of Styria, but was better suited to the more open border frontiers. The armor of seventeenth-century heavy cavalry appeared thick and clumsy; the shortcuts taken to facilitate production stripped the armor of its grace. Full armor was extremely rare. Most cavalry wore either half armor with open *Zischägge,* or, in the case of cuirassiers (horsemen with pistols), a very heavy three-quarter armor of proof [figure 18]. Even armor for horses was reduced to only a shaffron, at most. As in earlier years, light cavalry remained popular, but other horsemen wore merely a buff coat [figure 70], with or without a cuirass or perhaps an iron collar to protect the throat and upper chest. All cavalry except saber-wielding hussars carried cut-and-thrust swords [figure 69].

71
Attributed to Heinrich De
Veerle, *Portrait of Wolf von
Eggenberg,* c. 1680 [checklist
no. 191].

Wolf von Eggenberg
(c. 1580–1615), the nephew
of Ruprecht [figure 60], here
wears an armor that is probably
more imaginary than authentic.
Wolf was a rough-and-ready
military man with a distinguished career who, after losing
a leg in a skirmish with the
Ottomans, had a wooden
prosthesis made so that he
could continue to mount and
ride a horse. This portrait was
painted posthumously for the
Eggenberg family mausoleum.

As man-to-man sporting combats on foot within the lists and at the barriers lost favor, men turned to duels with swords, and later pistols, to settle matters of honor. With the decline of body armor, the ability to deliver a skillful thrust was crucial to battle and the mark of martial prowess. The need to properly wield a sword led to regional schools of swordsmanship. In the second half of the seventeenth century, the French school was preferred, with its emphasis on the thin, light small-sword used quickly and with great effect.

In the east, the troops of the empire continued along the reliable, rather conservative lines they had followed for so many years. Even in the 1680s and afterwards, heavy half armors of proof were widespread. High-ranking commanders such as Johann Georg III of Saxony and Markgraf Ludwig Wilhelm of Baden (the so-called Türkenlouis) wore such protection in their Turkish wars, and the final deliveries of similar armor to the Landeszeughaus were made in 1685. The last vestiges of armor died hard. Some units of Bavarian heavy cavalry that fought at the battle of Blenheim in 1704 wore half armors indistinguishable from those of a half century earlier, and European horsemen wore bulletproof breastplates during the Seven Years' War (1757–63).

By the beginning of the eighteenth century, armor had, for the most part, disappeared from European battlefields. But long after it fell from use, its dignified associations survived. Men of noble birth continued to have their portraits painted wearing traditional or highly elaborate and somewhat fanciful armors [figure 71], thus preserving for posterity all the status, the bearing, the martial prowess, and the bravery that man has associated with armor throughout its long and distinguished history.

ARMS, ARMOR, AND FINE ARTS

Peter Krenn

72
Lucas Cranach the Elder,
The Judgment of Paris, 1515
[checklist no. 61].

This is one of a number of autograph replicas by Lucas Cranach the Elder of this mythological scene. The early 16th-century armor of Paris is typical of the period, but Mercury's fantastic armor is merely Cranach's attempt to suggest the antique.

From the beginning of time, man has had a special relationship with arms, for they have been closely tied to his very existence. With his weapons he captured life-sustaining nourishment and protected his family, his people, and, indeed, his species, when their well-being was threatened. As a result, he associated many of the noblest expressions of human life—power and strength, bravery and self-sacrifice, loyalty and solidarity—with his arms. Over time, weapons assumed ideal and symbolic values above and beyond their material function. Homer described the tradition of preserving a weapon as a souvenir, a trophy, or an offering; as the legitimization of a claim; or even as a collectible object. Due to this urge to protect the souvenirs of important struggles, men preserved armaments in ecclesiastical, dynastic, and secular treasuries. One of the great historical European arms collections, the Landeszeughaus, or the Styrian State Armory of Graz, was saved from dissolution thanks to a conviction to preserve these arms and to document Styria's military achievement.

Likewise, for nearly as long as there have been weapons, craftsmen have wanted to decorate them. Throughout the history of arms, and reaching a high point during the Renaissance, a man's station, status, wealth, and personal taste determined how elegant and how exquisite his weapons would be. To be sure, a man's arms were an extension of his clothing and a distinguishing sign of his social position [figures 55, 73].

STYLISTIC AFFINITIES BETWEEN ARMS AND ART

Arms were always a part of man's search to embellish his world and to shape his surroundings according to a particular style. The creative energy of an era is as evident in its weapons as it is in other types of fine and applied art. For centuries decoration enhanced even the simplest and most common weapons, but with the mechanical mass production of

weapons in the nineteenth century, this idealistic and artistic dimension largely disappeared, and arms became indifferent instruments of war.

ARMOR AND ART HISTORY

For many years, art historians overlooked antique weapons in their research, neglecting important historical collections of arms with holdings dating from as early as the fourth century through the beginning of the nineteenth century. In 1936 Bruno Thomas, a distinguished art historian and later director of the famous arms collection of the Kunsthistorisches Museum in Vienna, challenged his colleagues to study the field of weapons because there was so much to be discovered from them. In his programmatic essay "Waffenkunde als Kunstwissenschaft" [The Aesthetics of Arms] (*Belvedere* XII, Vienna 1934/36), he explained that the art historian

73
Close Helmet for the Field, 1550–1570 [checklist no. 207]; Michel Witz the Younger, Burgonet from the Great Garniture for Field and Tournament of Kaspar Baron Völs-Schenkenberg, 1560 [checklist no. 96.1].

The close helmet was the knightly headpiece of the 16th century. It enclosed the head completely, yet provided a nearly ideal combination of protection, vision, and ventilation.

will value the suit of armor as a three-dimensional form, for it expresses the strong and clear intention of three-dimensionality, allowing the human body to appear idealized in rigid form, encased on all sides, and yet movable. He will see revealed in the etched images on suits of armor and staff weapons a vast quantity of unpublished graphic art, etching, and engraving. He will admire the art of the goldsmiths and iron cutters who decorated fencing weapons. He will understand and appreciate the relief sculpture on embossed parade weapons in the context of general sculptural development. He will assure arms a place in a future history of applied art, next to religious artifacts and beside courtly and bourgeois decorative art and household objects.

More than fifty years have passed since these words were written, and that goal has certainly not yet been reached, but we have come a good deal closer. Bruno Thomas himself contributed substantially to its realization, aided by his longtime colleague and successor Ortwin Gamber, with whom he collaborated on the articles "Harnischstudien" [Studies in Armor] that appeared in the *Jahrbuch des Kunsthistorischen Museums in Wien* from 1937 to 1955.

Their studies are exemplary demonstrations of how arms can be understood in terms of stylistic history and incorporated into the chronology of art history. Thomas and Gamber convincingly explained that rather than being mere accessories, weapons are in fact themselves artistic creations that reflect larger stylistic tendencies of a period. This idea was inspired by the writings of the art historian Alois Riegel (1858–1905), who proposed that whether working in the fine or decorative arts, artists of any given era share a common *Kunstwollen,* or "stylistic intent." In their articles, Thomas and Gamber pointed out stylistic relationships between arms and art that had previously gone unnoticed. For example, the knightly armor of the High Gothic period of the thirteenth and early fourteenth centuries consisted of a helm, which fully covered the head, and a long-sleeved mail shirt, over which was worn the richly pleated battle dress (surcoat), fashioned like the long outer garments of the time. The soldier's figure was thus largely concealed; his identity had to be expressed by heraldic devices on his helm and shield. Similarly, in the art of the same period, the curved, linear folds in the clothing concealed the shape of the figures. The knightly warrior in battle dress, on one hand, and the Gothic robed figure, on the other, reveal the same idealized incorporeality and the dominance of an abstract play of lines and symbolic references. Behind these stand the thoughts of medieval Platonism, which places the idea of a thing above its perceptible appearance.

Thomas and Gamber proceeded to trace the stylistic changes from

74
St. Florian, c. 1520 [checklist no. 63].

According to legend, St. Florian, the patron who protects against the threat of fire, extinguished a burning church with a single bucket of water. Here he performs his firefighting heroics wearing a transitional form of armor of the Maximilian period, similar to that of St. George [figures 31, 32].

the *Lentner,* or cloth-covered armor, which was already fitted to the waist and so emphasized the body, to complete plate armor, developed at the end of the fourteenth century. With its torso armor, its vambraces and leg harnesses, and its corresponding joint connections, plate armor clearly described the body parts and their functions. Plate armor, moreover, corresponded to the realism that was felt throughout Europe in the fifteenth century [figure 31].

An already well-known and generally accepted relationship exists between the German suit of armor from about 1460 to 1480, richly decorated with ridges, grooves, and points, and the similar details in the work of contemporary German Late Gothic artists such as Michel Pacher (c. 1435–1498) and Bernt Notke (c. 1440–1509), or even of Italian Renaissance painters such as Andrea del Verrocchio (c. 1435–1488) and Antonio Pollaiuolo (c. 1432–1498). Fluted armor, a creation of the early sixteenth century, is understood as part of the new plasticity of the German Renaissance, seen, for example, in the work of Albrecht Dürer (1471–1528), Hans Burgkmair (1473–1531), and Hans Holbein the Younger (1497/8–1543), as well as in the intricate creations of the Danube School artists such as Lucas Cranach the Elder (1472–1553) [figure 72], and Albrecht Altdorfer (c. 1480–1538). The influence of the articles by Thomas and Gamber is confirmed by the fact that, after 1945, historical arms were more often included in books on applied arts. Today they are even more readily included in large exhibitions that focus on the historical and artistic periods of a particular region.

ORNAMENTAL MOTIFS ON ARMS AND ARMOR

Even more clearly than in the basic shape of a suit of armor, a pistol stock, or a halberd head, the style of an era can be revealed through the decorative ornamental details that organize and embellish the object's surface. Factors such as the care of execution, the density of decoration, and the costliness of materials not only reveal the artistic period of a weapon, but also provide clues about the social station of its owner. The elongated form of most edged, staff, and percussion weapons and firearms—derived from the weapons' functions—offered little surface for decoration, but that very shape inspired the craftsman's imagination to create unusual solutions [figure 75]. For example, early Germanic and Scandinavian peoples used animal and wickerwork motifs, common decorations for their houses and ships, to decorate their sword grips and scabbards as well. Later, the architectural feature of Gothic tracery, which

76
Master "MR" (perhaps Martin
Rotschmied, Michel Roth, or
Martin Rotschuch), Morion,
c. 1575 [checklist no. 206].

The high comb of this helmet
is etched with arabesques;
abstract moresque-like motifs
decorate the skull and brim.

◀75
Halberd, late 16th century
[checklist no. 212]; Boar Spear,
1573 [checklist no. 210];
Halberd, late 16th century
[checklist no. 213]; Halberd,
late 16th century [checklist
no. 214].

delineated the designs of stained-glass windows, was also imitated by
craftsmen on maces and for the pierced ornamentation of spearheads,
spurs, and stirrups.

With the emergence of the Italian Renaissance and the spread of its
influence throughout Europe in the sixteenth century, the decoration of
weapons developed with particular intensity. Rediscovered antique motifs
encouraged artists to invent more extravagant designs. The new and
flourishing medium of prints helped to spread these ornamental patterns,
whether through individual sheets or entire books on ornamentation.
Four ornamental forms that made a triumphant advance in the sixteenth
century—the arabesque, the grotesque, scrolled decoration, and the
moresque—are all frequently represented on weapons.

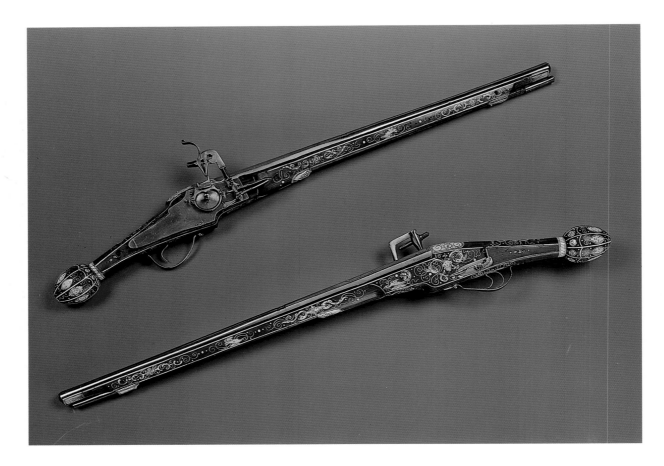

The arabesque was usually a symmetric, plastic, and naturalistic foliate tendril used in classical antiquity to decorate architectural elements. Early Italian Renaissance artists adopted this motif, and it was introduced to Germany about 1520. The arabesque spread further through ornamental prints by such German printmakers as Bartel Beham (1502–1540) and Heinrich Aldegrever (1502–c. 1560). Graceful arabesques were used in different variations as inlay work in the stocks of small firearms. They are also found as embossed decorative motifs on some parade armor of the sixteenth century, where they parallel gold and silver embroideries on garments [figure 76].

The grotesque is a more fanciful category of decoration that consists of combinations of symmetrically arranged foliate tendrils and various objects such as vases, candelabra, fruits, flowers, trophies, architectural elements, fabulous creatures, and animal and human figures [figures 78, 79]. This ancient form, developed in imperial Rome as architectural embellishment, was discovered there in the *Domus aurea* of Nero at the beginning of the sixteenth century. At that time, the *Domus aurea* was still underground, hence this decoration was named after *grotta*, the Italian for "cave." In 1511–14 Raphael made exemplary use of the grotesque in his series of murals for the *loggia* in the Vatican Palace, but the form of the

77
Nikolaus Klett, Pair of Wheel-lock Pistols, c. 1610 [checklist nos. 219.1–.2].

78, 79
Heinrich Aldegrever, *Ornament Arising from the Body of a Faun,* and *Ornament with Vase and Mask,* 1552 [checklist nos. 198 and 197].

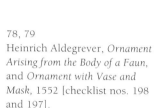

Aldegrever was one of the *Kleinmeister,* or artists who specialized in small prints such as these ornamental engravings, which served as models for craftsmen. The classical vase, mask, and faun motifs demonstrate the influence of the Italian Renaissance on German artists.

grotesque remained a favorite motif through the nineteenth century. Ornamental engravers in Italy and Germany have depicted the grotesque since its revival in the Renaissance, and it is found on arms dating to the second half of the sixteenth century. The grotesque's great popularity was in part due to its hybrid nature, which permitted artists and craftsmen working in a broad range of materials and techniques to vary the forms almost without limit. The fantastic diversity and refinement of the grotesque bestows upon objects the impression of heightened splendor.

Scrolled decoration was also in widespread use in architecture, the decorative arts, and graphic art. About 1550, ornamental prints carried scrolled designs from Italy to the Netherlands and Germany. The form's rolled and slotted bands appear on prints as cartouches and volute-like architectural elements that have a sculptural effect [figures 80, 81]. Scrolled decoration, despite its rather unwieldy nature, can be encountered on armors and shields of French and Flemish origin, sometimes combined with the grotesque. Frequently, however, it served as inlay work on the stocks of small firearms, where it found a natural place as a framing or accenting motif, similar to its use on furniture.

The moresque [figure 82] originated from the acanthus, the leaf used so often in antique decoration, but it was transformed in the East into a flat form with intricate surface decoration that became known in Italy in the fifteenth century through Islamic carpets, bookbindings, and glass. It was adopted in Italy and became known through ornamental prints, especially those by Francesco Pelegrino (d. 1552), who after 1530 belonged to the artistic circle at Fontainebleau. In 1546 in Nuremberg, the German ornamental printmaker Peter Flötner (1485–1546) compiled a book of moresque patterns, which was published in Zurich in 1549 and quickly spread throughout Europe. The silhouette-like, stylized foliate and tendril forms of the symmetrical moresque were engraved or etched onto armors [figure 83]. The moresque did not, however, attain the popularity of either scrolled decoration or the grotesque.

DECORATIVE TECHNIQUES

In addition to this new wealth of ornamental motifs, there were many decorative techniques that the skilled craftsman employed for arms. Line etching, developed during the late fifteenth century, used acid to assist the graving tool. With this method, the metal surface to be decorated is first covered with an acid-resistant protective medium, often wax, through which the etching needle can easily cut. Then a caustic acid is applied, which works into the exposed parts of the metal. After removing the protective coating, the etched design is blackened, making the design

80, 81
Virgil Solis, *Julius Caesar* and *Joshua* from a series of the *Nine Worthies,* early 1550s [checklist nos. 202 and 201].

In the early 1550s, Virgil Solis engraved a series of Nine Worthies, including characters of classical antiquity, the Old Testament, and the early Middle Ages. These portraits are framed by scrollwork ornaments and grotesque figures.

clearly visible. This technique for decorating arms was the precursor of printed etching, for if one were to rub an arms-etching with printer's ink, one could print it on paper.

It comes as no surprise that the discovery of the etching technique, first executed on iron plates and only later on copper or tin, can be attributed to the circle of arms-etcher Daniel Hopfer (c. 1470–1536), who came from a large Augsburg family of arms-etchers and graphic artists. Augsburg was not only an artistic center for painters, graphic artists, and goldsmiths, but it also produced the best gunsmiths and armorers, including the distinguished armorers of the Helmschmid family. Daniel Hopfer's achievement was widely recognized during his time, and in 1590 he was posthumously named as the inventor of the art of etching in an imperial patent of nobility bestowed upon his grandson Georg. On the whole, scholarship of arms etchings and other figured and ornamental arms decorations is still in its infancy. While Hopfer's contribution as a printmaker is generally acknowledged, his arms etchings are at least as important, and, like his prints, reveal the role that Italian ornamental motifs had on his transformation from a Late Gothic to a Renaissance

82
Christoph Jamnitzer, *Ornamental (Moresque) Band with Initials M A,* 1610 [checklist no. 204].

Jamnitzer, the son of Nuremberg's most important goldsmith, edited a volume of decorative etchings in 1610. The *Neue Groteskenbuch* [New Grotesque Book] includes works with fantastic themes.

artist. The etched motifs on the horse armor in the Landeszeughaus, for example, which were created shortly before 1510, show this important transition [figure 84]. Here he mixed intricate and fanciful Late Gothic foliate tendrils with Italianate fruit festoons that are clearly Renaissance in character. Although this armor does not appear in any inventory of Hopfer's work, it is more significant than many of his ornamental prints. In spite of recent advances in the scholarship of arms and armor, the armor decorations of this early Renaissance style innovator still have not been studied.

At the beginning of the sixteenth century, craftsmen expanded on the basic technique of etching and developed raised etching. In this variation, rather than the design being the intaglio, or recessed and darkened area, the design remains in slight relief and stands out against a background that is darkened by small etched dots. To accomplish this, the protective

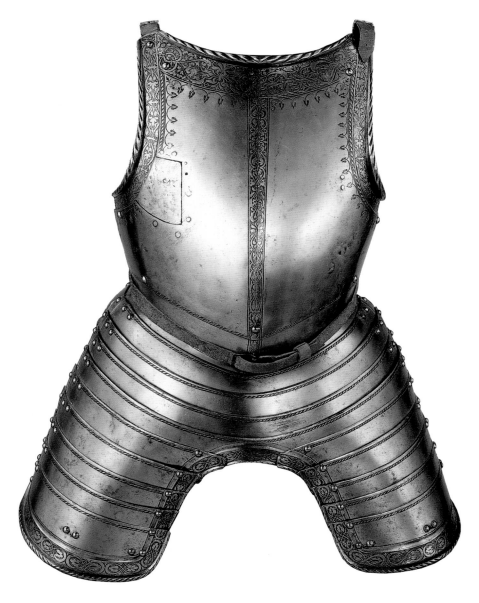

medium is applied with a brush to the parts that remain elevated, and is dotted with a quill over the background [figures 85, 86]. In Italy the background was crosshatched rather than dotted, making it possible to identify whether a decoration originated there.

Another technique of introducing a linear design onto the surface of a suit of armor, a shield, a sword, or a gun barrel was damascening [figure 30]. As its name implies, this technique originated in the East (Damascus is the root for the word; the German term is *Tauschierung,* from the Arabic *tausija,* meaning "decoration" or "coloring") and is achieved by beating a softer metal such as gold or silver into the harder iron. There are two methods for this. For the first, which was brought from Italy to Germany around 1520 and soon spread throughout Europe, the background surface is roughened with crosshatching. Then precious metal in the form of wire or small sheets is applied and the piece is smoothed to an even surface and polished. The second method is somewhat more difficult. The design is first cut into the iron surface with a graving tool. Gold, silver, or copper wire is then hammered into the recesses, holding the design more securely than in the other method and permitting it to remain raised.

In order to obtain the effect of color, various other methods were also employed, for example, painting with oil pigments or covering with fabric. The iron could also be heated to generate oxidation tints. With this technique, various colors could be achieved, from pale yellow at 428°F to purple at 518°F and dark blue at 590°F. If one wanted the coloration only on certain parts of the weapon, the oxidized surfaces could be removed by etching the metal with dilute acetic acid.

Various gilding techniques were more costly and also more tedious. In leaf-gilding, the gold leaf is laid on the freshly varnished iron surface; drying the varnish under pressure adheres the gold. In fire-gilding, the metal object is prepared with a copper solution before a gold and mercury

84
School of Konrad Seusenhofer, etched in the early style of Daniel Hopfer the Elder, Horse Armor (detail), 1505–10 [checklist no. 57.1].

amalgam is applied. Heating causes the mercury to evaporate, leaving the pure gold adhering to the metal. The gold-melting and enameling process is similar. For these, the gilded designs are first etched or engraved into the metal.

In addition to these methods of decorating the surface of an object, there were also some that transformed the object more substantially. Such was the ancient technique of embossing, or repoussé. It flourished anew in the sixteenth century, especially in connection with the *all'antica* style of armaments. In this technique, the design is first sketched on the object and is then punched and hammered from the inside to form a raised motif. The Landeszeughaus owns a beautiful example of this treatment in the three-quarter armor from about 1550 by Michel Witz the Younger [figure 87].

Especially in weapons, iron-cutting and iron-relief engraving facilitated pierced forms and reliefs on metal surfaces. Here, the ground was hollowed out with a chisel and worked with a punch and graving tool. These ornamentations were very common for sword and dagger hilts and were also used on small firearms [figure 88]. Related to this is pierced ornamentation, or fretwork, in which iron is perforated and cut out, a favorite technique in armors of the fifteenth and sixteenth centuries. Cutout tin patterns, which were applied to pistol stocks and powder bottles, also belong to this category.

Finally, the decorative techniques that flourished in the Renaissance and Baroque eras for other decorative arts were also used to embellish the wooden stocks of rifles, pistols, and crossbows. Most common was bone or ivory inlay, which was used in connection with bone engraving [figures 89, 90, 91]. Almost every small sixteenth-century firearm in the armory—and there are more than one thousand of them—is adorned with inlay. In this procedure, the design is engraved on a small plaque of bone and blackened. Then a section of wood is removed from the stock to accommodate the plaque, which is glued in place. In a similar method, bone and mother-of-pearl plaques were not only laid into the stock, but also fixed with metal pins.

The stocks themselves could also be carved from wood or ivory, a technique that demanded great skill. Stocks of small firearms, or even objects such as powder flasks and sword hilts, have been sculpted into fully three-dimensional creations.

85

85, 86
Field Armor (with detail of breastplate), 1540–1550 [checklist no. 72].

Many German and Austrian breastplates from the mid 16th century bear an etched crucifixion-and-kneeling-knight motif. It has been suggested that in some cases these depicted the armor's owner, making a personalized devotional image for a soldier to wear in battle.

Michel Witz the Younger, Black-and-White Three-quarter Armor for a Nobleman, c. 1550 [checklist no. 95].

Michel Witz was a master armorer who made this exquisite suit for an important client. This armor is decorated with a black-and-white finish, in which the craftsman alternated bright, polished surfaces with unpolished or otherwise darkened areas. In addition, the armor has been embossed, a process whereby the metal was punched and raised from within, producing a design in relief.

ARMS AND ARMOR IN ART

The representation of battle and armaments in the arts of painting, sculpture, printmaking, drawing, and other media is a nearly inexhaustible subject of study. Such representations parallel human history from the cave paintings of Stone Age man to the depiction of real or fictitious scenes of war and revolution in modern photographs and motion pictures. The greatest artists have created battle images of wide-ranging style and scope, and many of these are among the most outstanding works in the history of art.

In western European culture, the representation of war has had both a mythic and an actual dimension. Phidias, the renowned sculptor of the Acropolis, carved the battle of the Lapiths and Centaurs in the metopes of the Parthenon; the masters of the Hellenistic altar to Zeus in Pergamum showed the gods' tortured faces in the intensely dramatic frieze of the *gigantomachia* (the battle of giants). The Romans, on the other hand, always more inclined than their predecessors to record artistically the minute details of history, decorated the triumphal columns of Trajan and Marcus Aurelius with faithful representations of military campaigns. They are now prized as documents of the armaments of the empire and its enemies in the second century.

88

Wheel-lock Pistol (detail), 1575–1600 [checklist no. 162].

This doghead and pierced wheel cover is decorated with engraving and iron cutting.

89 ▶▶

Pair of Wheel-lock Pistols, c. 1575 [checklist nos. 217 and 218].

The blued barrels, as well as the cock, pan, and wheel cover, are engraved with foliate motifs consisting of wavy tendrils with short acanthus leaves emerging from vases and masks. The brown stocks are inlaid with staghorn. The same decoration is found on the cartridge box. The stockmaker may have based his design on engravings by Heinrich Aldegrever.

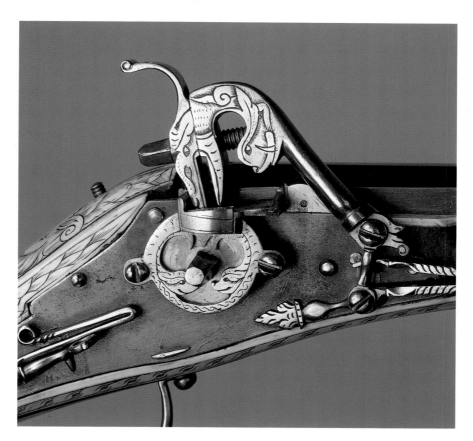

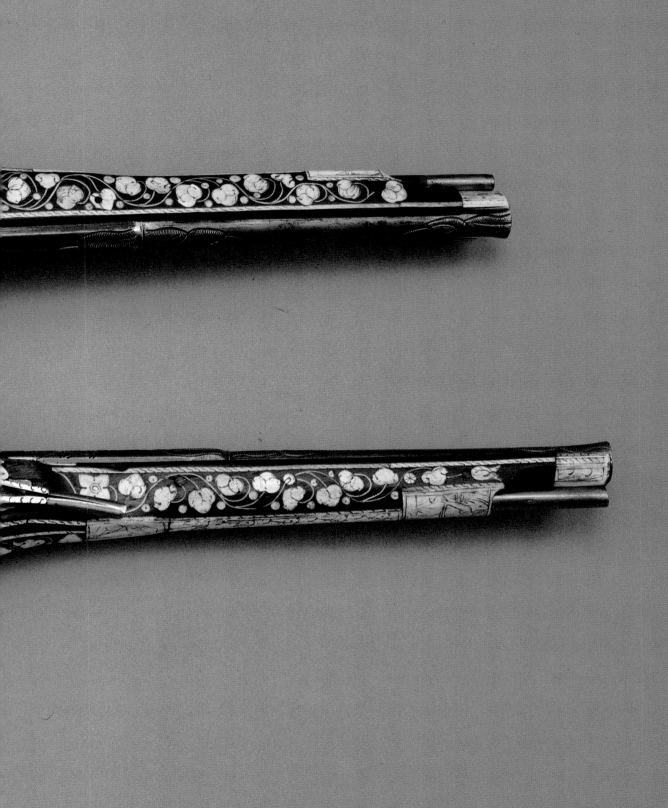

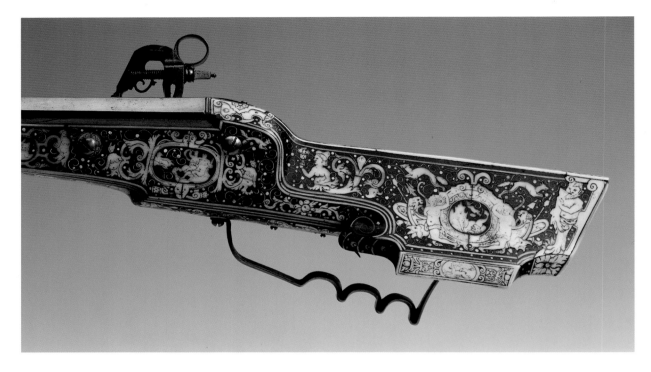

Since Roman times, in fact, the most important representations of arms in art are generally characterized by realism of observation—by what we now would recognize as a documentary impulse. The famous Bayeux tapestry, for instance, records the exploits of William the Conqueror, including his victory in 1066 at the Battle of Hastings, as a series of embroidered panels. Created only a short time after the events took place, this lively pictorial narrative is a unique document of the appearance and use of Norman and English armaments of the eleventh century, and modern historians of arms and art alike have cooperated to interpret its significance. Even in devotional images of the Late Gothic period, such as the *Votive Tablet of St. Lambrecht,* c. 1430, [figure 6] or in the panel from the somewhat provincial *Miraculous Altar of Mariazell,* [figure 11] painted around 1512 by an artist of the Danube School, the will to record the actuality of arms can be appreciated. Although both paintings were created as images of religious inspiration and propaganda, the weapons depicted and the action of battle help the modern viewer understand the function of armaments.

The development of pictorial perspective by painters of the fifteenth century makes their art particularly instructive to the modern student of arms and armor. Artists as different as the Florentines Andrea dell Castagno (1421?–1457) and Paolo Uccello (1396/7–1475), the Netherlandish painter Jan van Eyck (active 1422–1441), and the German Konrad Witz (1410/11–1444/46) treated armaments in pictorial terms that still

90
Master "MM" (barrelmaker) and Master "CO" (stockmaker), Wheel-lock Hunting Rifle, c. 1600 [checklist no. 227].

This German-type stock is richly inlaid with engraved late Renaissance-style staghorn decoration. The primary motifs are grotesques, foliate stripes, and tendrils; on the reverse are mythological scenes in rollwork frames depicting Perseus and Andromeda, Poseidon and Amphitrite, and Europa and the Bull. On top of the butt is the stockmaker's monogram, "CO."

91
Stock for a Hunting Rifle
(detail), 1600–1625 [checklist
no. 225].

Although the barrel and lock
are lost, this long stock is
remarkable, for it is the most
ornate in the Landeszeughaus.
Its lavishly dense and intricate
decoration includes tendrils,
grotesque motifs, allegorical
figures, and medallions with
views of a town.

seem wholly convincing to the modern viewer. Even today we can study
their paintings for clues about the history of arms. By the same token, we
can compare surviving elements of armor and their representation in
contemporaneous works of art—such as the hussar's shield perhaps made
in Hungary [figure 36] and a nearly identical shield carried by a soldier
in the Danube School panel painting *The Legend of St. Sigismund,* c. 1520,
by the Master of the Brucker Panel of St. Martin [figure 36].

The representation of armor is not always strictly historical, however.
When, about 1515, the German master Lucas Cranach the Elder
composed the *Judgment of Paris,* [figure 72] he considered it entirely
appropriate to clothe the sleeping Paris—a prince of ancient Troy—in
a faithful representation of a modern suit of armor. (By contrast, the
bearded figure of Mercury in the painting wears a fanciful armor,
combining ancient and modern forms, that Cranach deemed appropriate
for a demi-god.) An Italian painter of Cranach's time—Raphael, for
instance—would have been more likely to adhere faithfully to an
Arcadian tradition, and would have insisted on clothing the Trojan
shepherd-prince in a pastoral costume derived from antique statuary or
wall paintings. For the German-speaking painter of the early sixteenth
century, on the other hand, the association between princely grandeur
and arms and armor was taken almost as a matter of course.

It is in the German-speaking world of the Renaissance, therefore,
that some of the greatest representations of princely armor can be found.

In 1512 the Habsburg Emperor Maximilian I commissioned an ambitious series of woodblock prints and illustrated books to glorify his military achievements and the memory of his family. The works included illustrations to the propagandistic romances *Freydal, Theuerdank,* and *Weisskunig,* as well as the many woodblock prints that together comprise the *Triumphzug* (a triumphal chariot and procession), and the *Ehrenpforte* (a printed triumphal arch that celebrated Maximilian's dynasty). Following the instructions dictated by the emperor, these large and complex prints are overwhelmingly devoted to battle, the tournament, and the hunt, as well as to the diverse branches of arms production and of military science. The list of artists called to this undertaking includes many of the most important printmakers of the Northern Renaissance: along with Albrecht Dürer, Hans Burgkmair, and Albrecht Altdorfer, there were Jörg Kölderer (active 1497–1540), Hans Schäuffelein (c. 1483–1539/40), Leonhard Beck (1480–1542), and Jörg Breu (c. 1475–1537). Seldom have painters and graphic artists—even those who specialized in military subjects—come to terms as intensively with the weapons and military apparatus of their time as did the printmakers who worked on Maximilian's extravagant projects. Nor did the need for the exacting representation of such equipment impair their creative imagination. It was truly a lucky circumstance for the emperor that his reign coincided with the greatest period of German art.

The sixteenth-century proliferation of printed books created a demand for illustrations of all aspects of human endeavor, including illustrations of military figures such as those drawn and engraved for *Dess Neuwen Kunstbuchs* [New Art Book], by the Swiss-born Jost Amman [figures 64, 93]. An unknown copyist could turn to an illustration by Amman, a woodcut for a manual on courtly tournaments, as inspiration for a lively painting of *The Great Tournament in Vienna* [figure 37]. In fact, printed sourcebooks such as these disseminated the image of the modern soldier or man of arms to artists and craftsmen throughout Europe.

Thus the Dutch engraver Jacob Jacques de Gheyn (1565–1629) influenced the image of west and central European infantrymen of his time with the magnificent figures of his drill book from 1607 [figures 16, 17, 63]. Franz Hals (1581/5–1666) and Rembrandt (1606–1669), with their famous group portraits of civic militia, established monuments to the Dutch soldier and to the military way of thinking. Likewise Philips Wouwerman (1619–1668), in paintings such as his *Soldiers in Baggage Train,* [figure 70] codified for Europe in the seventeenth century the image of cavalry soldiers at camp in the field—a not infrequent incident in a

92

92
Modeled by Leonard Magt, cast by Stephan Godl, *Nude Warrior,* 1526 [checklist no. 67].

Godl moved from Nuremberg to Innsbruck in 1508 to cast handguns. By 1514, he and Magt were among the artists who designed and finished the mausoleum for Maximilian I in Innsbruck.
The warrior's pose is typical of Italian Renaissance figures, while the slender body and fine detail embody German Late Gothic elements.

century dominated by international war.

Of course, this brief survey can only mention some of the ways in which artists have treated the subject of armaments. But it is still clear that fifty years after his pioneering research, Bruno Thomas' challenge to art historians has been embraced. Historians no longer hesitate to approach the subject of arms and armor, for their history is now valued as being integral to that of both art and culture. Indeed, the study of arms and armor has been humanized in the best sense of the word.

GLOSSARY OF TERMS

Walter J. Karcheski, Jr.

almain collar ■ a form of neck defense often found on heavy infantry and light cavalry armors during the 16th and the first half of the 17th centuries with short, gutter-like laminated defenses called spaudlers to protect the upper arm.

armet ■ like the **close helmet** that replaced it, this is a closely fitting, knightly helmet that totally encases the head. It consists of a skull with neckplate and very deep cheekpieces that conform to the chin, where they overlap and lock together. This join is somewhat reinforced by the visor when it is lowered.

backplate ■ plate armor for the back, frequently with attached plates for the lower-back region.

bandoleer ■ a firearms accessory used from the first half of the 16th century. It consists of a wide leather strap worn across the body, from which are suspended waterproofed bottles or boxes with premeasured charges for the firearm.

barbut ■ a deep, one-piece helmet used from the second half of the 14th until the late 15th centuries. In its classic form it is reminiscent of the ancient Greek "Corinthian" helmet and has a T-shaped facial opening.

bard ■ a comprehensive name for armor protecting the horse. Horse armor made of **mail** or soft armor is called a trapper. A full plate bard consisted of a shaffron (horse-head defense), crinet (neck armor), peytral (chest armor), flanchards (plates at the sides, below the saddle), and crupper (armor for the hindquarters).

basnet ■ a helmet widely used during the 14th and 15th centuries. The skull is generally deep and either pointed, ogival, or egg-shaped, usually with a visor hinged at either the brow or the temples. Basnets often have a

94, 95
Skylit Trellis, 1574 [checklist no. 55].

This trellis once hung above the irongate (*Eisernes Tor*) at the southern entrance to the city of Graz. The five decorative zones of the gate are filled with Renaissance spiral motifs. The Habsburg double eagle, cut out of iron sheet and painted gold bronze, is in the central section; two Styrian panthers are in flanking sections.

mail neckpiece defending the throat and neck, although some later types substitute deep plates, with the helmet resting on the shoulders.

bevor ■ that element of armor for the lower face and throat. The term can refer to separate pieces worn with helmets, such as a **sallet** and a **burgonet** (here usually called a **buffe**), or it can indicate that portion of a close helmet that is shaped to the chin and jaw, working at a com-mon set of pivots at the temple.

black-and-white armor ■ term used to describe a decorative treatment obtained from alternate polished ("white") and darkened ("black") surfaces on an armor. Blackening could be obtained by leaving the surface semi-finished (hammer-rough), by heat and oil treatments, or more often, by black paint.

boar spear ■ a type of spear with a broad, leaf-shaped blade and often a cross-toggle below. Originally a hunting arm, its form was sometimes used by horsemen and infantry, particularly by guards, as the wide head readily lent itself to decoration.

breastplate ■ the element of plate armor protecting the chest and abdomen. The breastplate was often worn with a **backplate,** to which it was attached by leather straps and buckles.

brigandine ■ the lighter, vest-like version of the **coat-of-plates.** Extremely popular with footsoldiers during the 15th century, it remained in use until almost the end of the 16th century. Some examples have sleeves made in the same manner as the body armor.

broadsword ■ a straight-bladed, double-edged weapon capable of being wielded with one hand. Designed to deal cutting blows, the broadsword was very popular with European heavy cavalry until the early part of the 19th century.

buff coat ■ a long, thick leather jacket, with or without sleeves, worn either with iron armor or by itself as a form of soft armor. The buff coat was popular from the late 16th through the 17th centuries.

buffe ■ a separate element of armor, usually detachable, that was worn with the open **burgonet** to provide a defense for the face. Some forms consist of multiple laminations that could be raised or lowered at will (then called a "falling-buffe").

burgonet ■ a comfortable, light, open headpiece with a peak or fall over the brow, and hinged cheekpieces. Used by infantry and cavalry, it could be made into a closed burgonet by use of a **buffe**. The burgonet was popular throughout the 16th and into the 17th centuries. Later examples often have cheekpieces so deep that they overlap and form a closed head-piece.

cabasset ■ a light, open headpiece sometimes called a "Spanish morion." The cabasset has an almond-shaped skull terminating in a short, rear-wardly angled stalk, with a narrow, flat brim at the base of the skull. Closely related is the variant called the comb-cap, which has a comb in place of the stalk. The cabasset was very popular with footsoldiers and some cavalry, including the harquebusiers. (See also **morion.**)

carbine ■ a short, lightweight firearm developed from the **harquebus** and designed for cavalry. It was often fitted with a sling and swivel for carrying.

close helmet ■ a helmet developed at the beginning of the 16th century. This helmet closely and entirely encases the head. Unlike the **armet,** all its elements work on a common set of pivots at the temples, and it has no cheekpieces. The most common form had gorget plates at the neck, while an alternate version was finished in a hollow flange that locked over the collar of the armor.

coat-of-plates ■ a type of torso armor used from the end of the 12th until the early 15th centuries. It consists of iron plates covered by a fabric or leather casing. (See also **brigandine.**)

codpiece ■ an element of armor protecting the male genitals. The cod-piece followed civilian costume fashion of the period, and some examples are quite elaborate and graphic.

collar (or gorget) ■ armor that encloses the throat and the upper part of the torso, thus providing vital linkage between helmet and **cuirass.** Gor-gets were simplified during the decline of armor, and were worn alone or to supplement a **buff coat.** In its final form, it evolved into a crescent-shaped plate suspended from the neck to signify an officer's rank. (See also **almain collar.**)

crossbow ■ a powerful but relatively slow-firing missile weapon used by infantry. The bow is perpend.icularly mounted at the end of a stock, and is drawn by handpower or with mechanical assistance. After the mid 16th century, the crossbow was generally used only for sport.

crupper ■ see **bard**

cuirass ■ the combination of breast- and backplates.

cuirassier ■ a heavy cavalryman of the late 16th to the first half of the 17th century. The cuirassier wore a bulletproof, **three-quarter armor** with a **close helmet** or *Zischägge,* and he was armed with pistols and a sword.

culverin ■ an artillery piece of the 15th through 17th centuries. The culverin was of the same caliber as a cannon, but its barrel was longer and heavier.

estoc ■ a cut-and-thrust sword with a stiff, narrow blade that was designed to penetrate armor. Its name was derived from the French word for "to thrust."

falconet ■ a light field gun firing solid shot weighing between one and three pounds.

flanchards ■ see **bard**

flintlock ■ the last and best of the spark-striking ignition systems. The flintlock is first recorded in the 16th century, and it did not become obsolete until the 19th century. In its perfected form, pressure on the trigger causes the engaged cock with flint to snap forward, sharply striking a combined pan-cover and steel. Hitting the vertical face of the steel, the flint gives off a shower of sparks, while at the same time the force of the cock impact pushes the pan-cover and steel away, exposing the priming powder to the sparks and thus igniting it.

gauntlets ■ leather-lined, armored gloves for the hands. Like **sabatons,** these can be of **mail,** mail and plate, or laminated plate. Plate gauntlets were made in mitten and fingered forms. Specialized gauntlets were made for jousting, foot combat, and duelling. Elbow gauntlets have elongated cuffs, thus serving as armor for the forearm.

glaive ■ a hafted weapon with a long, knife-like head fitted in line with the shaft.

gorget ■ see **collar**

Hakenbüchse ■ German name for early firearms (literally, "hook-gun," referring to the downward-projecting lug of the barrel, which served as an anti-recoil device).

halberd ■ an infantry staff weapon that combines an axblade, a spike, and a hook-like fluke in one head. The name is derived from the German words *Halm* ("staff") and *Barte* ("ax").

half armor ■ armor extending only to the hip. It is sometimes fitted with **tassets,** which run down the thigh but stop above the knee.

hand-and-a-half sword (or "bastard" sword) ■ a sword that is somewhat longer than the single-hand **broadsword,** yet smaller than a **two-handed sword.** Although light enough to be used in one hand, for increased power its grip can accommodate several fingers of the other hand.

harness ■ a period term for armor in general.

harquebus (arquebus) ■ derived from *Hakenbüchse.* The term was later used generically to describe a gun lighter than the musket.

hauberk ■ The medieval French name for a long shirt of **mail** extending to below-knee level. The hauberk was replaced by a shorter version, the *haubergeon.*

joust ■ a sporting combat between two individuals.

kettle hat ■ a headpiece widely used by infantry and as an alternative to the helm during the Middle Ages. Beginning in the 16th century, the kettle hat was increasingly employed in siege warfare and, suitably bulletproofed, was so used well into the 17th century.

lance-rest (or rest of the lance) ■ a shock-absorbing bracket found on the breastplate of armors that were designed to accommodate the lance during field or sporting combat on horseback. Some forms are fixed by a staple and pins, while others could be pivoted when the lance was not in use.

lists ■ the designated, sometimes fenced-in area where sporting foot and mounted combats occurred.

linstock ■ a long holder for slow-match, used by gunners until the 19th century. Some linstocks are combined with a spearhead as a means of self-defense.

mace ■ a club-like percussion weapon, most often with an iron head, that can be of various forms but usually flanged. In eastern Europe maces often followed Islamic fashion and featured rounded or bulbous heads.

mail ■ an ancient type of body armor comprised of interlocking metal rings, generally of iron or steel, that form a closely spaced network. Mail is often incorrectly referred to as "chain mail." (See also **hauberk**.)

man-at-arms ■ a non-knightly member of the heavy cavalry.

matchlock ■ the first system of mechanically applying ignition to a firearm in which a length of smoldering slow-match is held in the jaws of a cock or serpentine. Manual pressure on a trigger or button presses the match into the pan of priming powder, discharging the main charge in the barrel.

morion ■ a light, open helmet that was used throughout the 16th century by European infantry and light horsemen. The classic form has a rounded skull with a tall comb that reaches from front to rear, and a curved brim that sweeps up into pointed ends.

musket ■ a heavy, long-barreled firearm that replaced the **harquebus** as the chief weapon of infantry. The muskets dating from the period under discussion are generally of **matchlock** ignition and were fired from a forked rest to help support the barrel's weight.

partisan ■ an infantry staff weapon with a straight, double-edged central blade flanked at its base by curved lugs. The expanse of the head invited decoration, making the partisan a popular ceremonial arm for officers and body guards.

pauldron ■ a defense for the shoulder and upper arm.

pennon ■ a triangular streamer attached to a lance shaft just below the metal point.

peytral ■ see **bard**

pike ■ a spear-like thrusting arm of specialist infantry. Pikes were used in great numbers and averaged some 14 to 20 feet in length.

Pluderhose ■ the German name for the extremely baggy, full "puffed and slashed" breeches worn in central Europe during the 16th century.

plug bayonet ■ a close-defense, dagger-like weapon with a tapered grip that is pressed into the muzzle of a **musket.** This effectively made each musketeer his own pikeman, thus increasing the number of firearm-carrying infantry in a unit. A plugged muzzle, however, could be neither loaded nor fired, so the plug bayonet was later replaced by a socketed type that locked onto the muzzle.

polearms ■ a generic name for the group of shafted weapons generally requiring the use of both hands and employed almost exclusively by fighters on foot.

quintain ■ a term describing both the event and the target in a training activity, later purely a test of equestrian skill, in which a single horseman with lance attempted to strike a figure that often represented an Ottoman warrior. If the target was hit poorly, the figure swung about and buffeted the rider as he passed.

rifling ■ spiraled grooving within the barrel of a firearm. Properly cut, rifling imparts a flight-stabilizing spin to a projectile.

rondache ■ the French term for a circular shield worn on the arm and used into the 17th century.

sabatons ■ armor for the feet. These could be of **mail,** mail with a plate toe cap, or laminated plates. Sabatons became increasingly rare during the second half of the 16th century, when armor for the lower leg was usually omitted. Like breastplates, sabatons generally reflect the prevailing civilian fashions.

saber ■ a curved cutting sword used almost exclusively by cavalry.

sallet ■ a semi-open helmet with rounded skull, often drawn out in a tail that is often laminated. Sallets were made with and without visors but, unless supplemented by a **bevor,** they usually provided protection only to the upper part of the face. Later forms of the sallet that combined a pivoted bevor and visor evolved into the **close helmet.**

shaffron ■ see **bard**

spanner ■ the arming wrench or key for a wheel-lock gun.

spaudlers ■ see **almain collar**

tassets ■ plates suspended from a breastplate by rivets or straps and buckles, which cover the gap between the bottom of the breastplate and the top of the thigh armor. Tassets can be of one piece or laminated.

three-quarter armor ■ a form of armor without metal defenses for the lower legs and feet. It was usually worn with leather boots.

tilt ■ the fence-like barrier separating the pair of participants in certain varieties of joust.

tilting-target (targe) ■ a heavy, shield-like reinforcing plate for tilting use. The tilting-target was bolted to the front left shoulder and chest region of an armor. Some forms are smooth while others have applied metal trelliswork on the surface.

tournament (tourney) ■ group sporting combats, on horse or on foot.

trapper ■ see **bard**

two-handed sword ■ a large infantry sword, up to 6 feet in length. Although relatively lightweight (8 to 10 pounds), it required both hands and special training for effective use. Like many other arms, it became a weapon for use in ceremonies and by bodyguards.

vamplate ■ the plate of iron or steel mounted on the shaft of a lance, just forward of the hand, which it protects.

wheel-lock ■ earliest of the spark-striking ignitions, and of unknown origin. A pre-set, spring-tensioned wheel revolves rapidly when the trigger is pulled, rotating against a piece of iron pyrite held in the jaws of a movable cock. This produces sparks and, at the same time, a pan cover slides open, exposing the priming powder. The sparks set off this powder and, in turn, the main charge.

Zischägge ■ German translation of the Turkish *shishak* helmet (itself a reference to a pointed skull). Perhaps of Balkan origin and perfected by Ottoman armorers, this helmet was extremely popular in Europe from the second half of the 16th through the first half of the 17th centuries. The *Zischägge* typically has a hemispherical skull and a fall with nasal guard, cheekpieces, and a deep laminated (or pseudo-laminated) nape defense or tail.

CHECKLIST OF THE EXHIBITION

Peter Krenn

Christine Rabensteiner

edited by
Walter J. Karcheski, Jr.
and Ann Wood

96
Bodyguard to Count Niklas Zrinyi, c. 1566 [checklist no. 77.3].

Checklist dimensions are given in inches followed by centimeters in parentheses. All armor dimensions are approximate and in some cases are representative averages of a group of similar elements.

1
Attributed to Johann Jakob Schoy,
Austrian (1686–1733)
Styrian Panther
Early eighteenth century
Limewood, paint, and gilt
34⅝ x 24 x 10⅜ (88 x 61 x 26.4)
Joanneum Graz, Alte Galerie, P 288

2
Attributed to Johann Jakob Schoy,
Austrian (1686–1733)
Styrian Panther
Early eighteenth century
Limewood, paint, and gilt
32⅝ x 25 x 9⅝ (83 x 63.5 x 24.5)
Joanneum Graz, Alte Galerie, P 289

3
Cuirass for Cavalry
c. 1620
Made in Graz
Iron and leather
Breastplate 15½ x 13⅛ (39.3 x 33.2)
Joanneum Graz, Landeszeughaus, A 2971

4
Cuirass for Cavalry
c. 1620
Made in Graz
Iron and leather
Breastplate 15½ x 13⅛ (39.3 x 33.2)
Joanneum Graz, Landeszeughaus, A 2972

5
Cuirass for Cavalry
c. 1620
Made in Graz
Iron and leather
Breastplate 15½ x 13⅛ (39.3 x 33.2)
Joanneum Graz, Landeszeughaus, A 2973

6
Cuirass for Cavalry
c. 1620
Made in Graz
Iron and leather
Breastplate 15½ x 13⅛ (39.3 x 33.2)
Joanneum Graz, Landeszeughaus, A 2974

7
Cuirass for Cavalry
c. 1620
Made in Graz
Iron and leather
Breastplate 15½ x 13⅛ (39.3 x 33.2)
Joanneum Graz, Landeszeughaus, A 2975

8
Cuirass for Cavalry
c. 1620
Made in Graz
Iron and leather
Breastplate 15½ x 13⅛ (39.3 x 33.2)
Joanneum Graz, Landeszeughaus, A 2976

9
Cuirass for Cavalry
c. 1620
Made in Graz
Iron and leather
Breastplate 15½ x 13⅛ (39.3 x 33.2)
Joanneum Graz, Landeszeughaus, A 2977

10
Cuirass for Cavalry
c. 1620
Made in Graz
Iron and leather
Breastplate 15½ x 13⅛ (39.3 x 33.2)
Joanneum Graz, Landeszeughaus, A 2978

11
Cuirass for Cavalry
c. 1620
Made in Graz
Iron and leather
Breastplate 15½ x 13⅛ (39.3 x 33.2)
Joanneum Graz, Landeszeughaus, A 2979

12
Cuirass for Cavalry
c. 1620
Made in Graz
Iron and leather
Breastplate 15½ x 13⅛ (39.3 x 33.2)
Joanneum Graz, Landeszeughaus, A 2980

13
Cuirass for Cavalry
c. 1620
Made in Graz
Iron and leather
Breastplate 15½ x 13⅛ (39.3 x 33.2)
Joanneum Graz, Landeszeughaus, A 3020

14
Cuirass for Cavalry
c. 1620
Made in Graz
Iron and leather
Breastplate 15½ x 13⅛ (39.3 x 33.2)
Joanneum Graz, Landeszeughaus, A 3027

15
Cuirass for Cavalry
c. 1620
Made in Graz
Iron and leather
Breastplate 15½ x 13⅛ (39.3 x 33.2)
Joanneum Graz, Landeszeughaus, A 3086

16
Cuirass for Cavalry
c. 1620
Made in Graz
Iron and leather
Breastplate 15½ x 13⅛ (39.3 x 33.2)
Joanneum Graz, Landeszeughaus, A 3087

17
Cuirass for Cavalry
c. 1620
Made in Graz
Iron and leather
Breastplate 15½ x 13⅛ (39.3 x 33.2)
Joanneum Graz, Landeszeughaus, A 3088

18
Cuirass for Cavalry
c. 1620
Made in Graz
Iron and leather
Breastplate 15½ x 13⅛ (39.3 x 33.2)
Joanneum Graz, Landeszeughaus, A 3089

19
Cuirass for Cavalry
c. 1620
Made in Graz
Iron and leather
Breastplate 15½ x 13⅛ (39.3 x 33.2)
Joanneum Graz, Landeszeughaus, A 3036

20
Cuirass for Cavalry
c. 1620
Made in Graz
Iron and leather
Breastplate 15½ x 13⅛ (39.3 x 33.2)
Joanneum Graz, Landeszeughaus, A 3038

21
Cuirass for Cavalry
c. 1620
Made in Graz
Iron and leather
Breastplate 15½ x 13⅛ (39.3 x 33.2)
Joanneum Graz, Landeszeughaus, A 3041

22
Cuirass for Cavalry
c. 1620
Made in Graz
Iron and leather
Breastplate 15½ x 13⅛ (39.3 x 33.2)
Joanneum Graz, Landeszeughaus, A 3057

23
Hungarian-style Helmet *(Zischägge)*
c. 1620
Made in Graz
Iron, leather, and brass
12⅝ x 7¾ (32 x 19.5)
Joanneum Graz, Landeszeughaus, A 1277

24
Hungarian-style Helmet (*Zischägge*)
c. 1620
Made in Graz
Iron, leather, and brass
12⅝ x 7¼ (32 x 19.5)
Joanneum Graz, Landeszeughaus, A 1289

25
Hungarian-style Helmet (*Zischägge*)
c. 1620
Made in Graz
Iron, leather, and brass
12⅝ x 7¼ (32 x 19.5)
Joanneum Graz, Landeszeughaus, A 1247

26
Hungarian-style Helmet (*Zischägge*)
c. 1620
Made in Graz
Iron, leather, and brass
12⅝ x 7¼ (32 x 19.5)
Joanneum Graz, Landeszeughaus, A 1248

27
Hungarian-style Helmet (*Zischägge*)
c. 1620
Made in Graz
Iron, leather, and brass
12⅝ x 7¼ (32 x 19.5)
Joanneum Graz, Landeszeughaus, A 1250

28
Hungarian-style Helmet (*Zischägge*)
c. 1620
Made in Graz
Iron, leather, and brass
12⅝ x 7¼ (32 x 19.5)
Joanneum Graz, Landeszeughaus, A 1252

29
Hungarian-style Helmet (*Zischägge*)
c. 1620
Made in Graz
Iron, leather, and brass
12⅝ x 7¼ (32 x 19.5)
Joanneum Graz, Landeszeughaus, A 1253

30
Hungarian-style Helmet (*Zischägge*)
c. 1620
Made in Graz
Iron, leather, and brass
12⅝ x 7¼ (32 x 19.5)
Joanneum Graz, Landeszeughaus, A 1294

31
Hungarian-style Helmet (*Zischägge*)
c. 1620
Made in Graz
Iron, leather, and brass
12⅝ x 7¼ (32 x 19.5)
Joanneum Graz, Landeszeughaus, A 1255

32
Hungarian-style Helmet (*Zischägge*)
c. 1620
Made in Graz
Iron, leather, and brass
12⅝ x 7¼ (32 x 19.5)
Joanneum Graz, Landeszeughaus, A 1256

33
Hungarian-style Helmet (*Zischägge*)
c. 1620
Made in Graz
Iron, leather, and brass
12⅝ x 7¼ (32 x 19.5)
Joanneum Graz, Landeszeughaus, A 1280

34
Hungarian-style Helmet (*Zischägge*)
c. 1620
Made in Graz
Iron, leather, and brass
12⅝ x 7¼ (32 x 19.5)
Joanneum Graz, Landeszeughaus, A 1291

35
Hungarian-style Helmet (*Zischägge*)
c. 1620
Made in Graz
Iron, leather, and brass
12⅝ x 7¼ (32 x 19.5)
Joanneum Graz, Landeszeughaus, A 1279

36
Hungarian-style Helmet (*Zischägge*)
c. 1620
Made in Graz
Iron, leather, and brass
12⅝ x 7¼ (32 x 19.5)
Joanneum Graz, Landeszeughaus, A 1281

37
Hungarian-style Helmet (*Zischägge*)
c. 1620
Made in Graz
Iron, leather, and brass
12⅝ x 7¼ (32 x 19.5)
Joanneum Graz, Landeszeughaus, A 1282

38
Hungarian-style Helmet *(Zischägge)*
c. 1620
Made in Graz
Iron, leather, and brass
12⅝ x 7¾ (32 x 19.5)
Joanneum Graz, Landeszeughaus, A 1283

39
Hungarian-style Helmet *(Zischägge)*
c. 1620
Made in Graz
Iron, leather, and brass
12⅝ x 7¾ (32 x 19.5)
Joanneum Graz, Landeszeughaus, A 1284

40
Hungarian-style Helmet *(Zischägge)*
c. 1620
Made in Graz
Iron, leather, and brass
12⅝ x 7¾ (32 x 19.5)
Joanneum Graz, Landeszeughaus, A 1285

41
Hungarian-style Helmet *(Zischägge)*
c. 1620
Made in Graz
Iron, leather, and brass
12⅝ x 7¾ (32 x 19.5)
Joanneum Graz, Landeszeughaus, A 1286

42
Hungarian-style Helmet *(Zischägge)*
c. 1620
Made in Graz
Iron, leather, and brass
12⅝ x 7¾ (32 x 19.5)
Joanneum Graz, Landeszeughaus, A 1287

43
Master of the Votive Tablet of St. Lambrecht
Votive Tablet of St. Lambrecht
c. 1430
Probably made in Styria
Distemper on pine
31⅛ x 65¾ x 1¾ (79 x 167 x 4.5)
Stift St. Lambrecht, St. Lambrecht, Styria, AG L 12

45
Mail Cape
1500–1550
Probably made in Styria
Iron and brass
H. 16⅞ (43)
Joanneum Graz, Landeszeughaus, PZ 137

47
Cut-and-Thrust Sword
Fourteenth century
Probably made in Styria
Iron and brass
40⅜ x 8⅝ x 1⅜ (102.5 x 21.8 x 3.3)
Joanneum Graz, Landeszeughaus, BL 2228

48
Thrusting Sword
Fifteenth century
Probably made in Styria
Iron
47⅞ x 10⅛ x 1¾ (121.5 x 25.7 x 4.5)
Joanneum Graz, Landeszeughaus, BL 2227

49
Left Stirrup
Fifteenth century
Probably made in Styria
Wrought iron
6 x 4⅞ x 2⅜ (15.3 x 12.5 x 5.9)
Joanneum Graz, Abteilung für Kunstgewerbe, AK 1643

50
Spur
Fifteenth century
Probably made in Styria
Wrought iron
7⅝ x 3⅜ x 2⅛ (19.2 x 8.4 x 5.4)
Joanneum Graz, Abteilung für Kunstgewerbe, AK 803

51
Georg Matthäus Vischer, Austrian (1628–1696)
Map of Styria formed as the Head of Mars, God of War
1681
Made in Tyrol
Hand-colored engraving on paper mounted on canvas
48⅝ x 54⅛ x 1 (123.5 x 137.5 x 2.5)
Joanneum Graz, Abteilung für Kunstgewerbe, AK 0944

52
Andreas Trost, Austrian (d. 1708)
View of City and Fortress of Graz
1703
Engraving on paper
20½ x 32⅝ (52.2 x 83)
Joanneum Graz, Abteilung Schloss Eggenberg, AE EG 758

53
Georg Matthäus Vischer,
Austrian (1628–1696)
Topographia Ducatus Stiriae
1681
Engraving on paper
Book 6⅝ x 11⅝ x 3¾ (16.7 x 29.5 x 9.5)
Joanneum Graz, Abteilung für
Kunstgewerbe, AK BI 580

54
Andreas Wickert the Elder,
German (1600–1661)
Chalice in the Shape of an Ostrich
c. 1650
Made in Augsburg
Silver and gilt
18⅞ x 7⅞ x 9½ (48 x 19.8 x 24.2)
Joanneum Graz, Abteilung für
Kunstgewerbe, AK 25.768

55
Skylight Trellis with Habsburg Double
Eagle and Styrian Panthers
1574
Made in Styria
Wrought iron and gilt
92⅛ x 128⅞ x 3¼ (234 x 327.5 x 8)
Joanneum Graz, Abteilung für
Kunstgewerbe, AK 761

56
The Turk of Saurau Palace
c. 1600
Made in Graz
Unidentified wood and paint
47¼ x 53⅛ x 17¾ (120 x 135 x 45)
Private collection, Graz

57.1
School of Konrad Seusenhofer,
Austrian (active 1500–1517)
Etched decoration in the early style of
Daniel Hopfer the Elder, Augsburg
(1470–1536)
Horse Armor
1505–10
Probably made in Innsbruck
Iron and leather
89¾ x 33⅞ x 55⅛ (228 x 86 x 140)
Joanneum Graz, Landeszeughaus, 1401

57.2
Saddle and Stirrups
1530–1540
Probably made in Germany or Austria
Iron and leather
Joanneum Graz, Landeszeughaus,
1401a, 1401b

58
Field Armor of the "Maximilian" form
(consisting of field helmet, collar, breastplate, backplate, pauldrons, vambraces, and leg harnesses with broad sabatons)
c. 1520
Made in Nuremberg
Iron and leather
Breastplate 16⅞ x 14½ (42.9 x 36.8)
Joanneum Graz, Landeszeughaus,
1219, 1221 B, 1223, 1224, 1245

59
Danube School
Panel from the *Miraculous Altar of Mariazell*, so-called "Small Miraculous Altar of Mariazell"
1512
Oil and distemper on pine
34¼ x 25¼ x 1⅝ (87 x 64 x 4)
Joanneum Graz, Alte Galerie, AG 386

60
Hans Maystetter,
Austrian, (active 1508–1533)
Field Armor of the "Maximilian" form
(consisting of close helmet with rondel, collar, breastplate with folding lance-rest and riveted tassets, backplate, pauldrons with haute pieces, vambraces, and leg harness with broad sabatons)
1510–11
Made in Innsbruck or Graz
Iron and leather
Breastplate 20⅞ x 18⅛ (53 x 46)
Joanneum Graz, Landeszeughaus, 1400

61
Lucas Cranach the Elder,
German (1472–1553)
The Judgment of Paris
1515
Oil distemper on limewood
34½ x 23¼ x 1 (87.5 x 59 x 2.5)
Joanneum Graz, Alte Galerie, AG 107

62
Workshop in the town of Villach
in Carinthia, Austria
St. George
c. 1520
Wood and paint
H. 55⅛ (140)
Filialkirche St. Leonhard, Murau

63
St. Florian
c. 1520 with later restoration
Made in Carinthia
Limewood, paint, and seventeenth-century gilt
42½ x 14⅝ x 11 (108 x 37 x 28)
Joanneum Graz, Alte Galerie, AG P 113

64
Danube School, Master of the Brucker Panel of St. Martin
Panel from the *Legend of St. Sigismund*
c. 1520
Made in Styria
Distemper on spruce
37 x 18⅛ (94 x 46)
Joanneum Graz, Alte Galerie, AG 351

65
Shield for a Hussar
Early sixteenth century
Probably made in Hungary
Birch(?), leather, iron, and paint
29½ x 22⅝ x 3⅞ (75 x 57.5 x 10)
Joanneum Graz, Landeszeughaus, A 2756

66
Saber with Scabbard
1550–1600
Probably made in Styria
Iron, leather, wood, and brass
Saber 35½ x 5½ x 1⅛ (90.2 x 14 x 2.8)
Scabbard 32¼ x 2⅜ x 1¼ (82 x 6 x 3)
Joanneum Graz, Landeszeughaus, BL 182

67
Modeled by Leonard Magt, German (d. 1532)
Cast by Stephan Godl, Austrian (d. 1534)
Nude Warrior
1526
Made in Innsbruck
Bronze
21¼ x 11¼ x 6⅛ (54 x 28.5 x 15.5)
Joanneum Graz, Alte Galerie, AG P 120

68.1
Perhaps Sebald Pögl, Austrian (c. 1465–1528)
Barrel for Light Field Gun (falconet)
Early sixteenth century
Made in Thörl, Styria
Wrought iron
L. 102⅜ (260)
Joanneum Graz, Landeszeughaus, G 376

68.2
Carriage for Light Field Gun (falconet)
Late sixteenth century
Larch and ash (wheels)
Carriage 83½ x 31⅞ (212 x 81)
Wheels dia. 43¼ (110)
Joanneum Graz, Landeszeughaus, G 377

68.3
Rammer and Brush for Light Field Gun (falconet)
Early sixteenth century
Wood, metal, and fiber
L. 85¼ (216.5)
Joanneum Graz, Landeszeughaus, G 440

68.4
Linstock (match holder) for Light Field Gun (falconet)
Early sixteenth century
Wood and metal
L. 57½ (146)
Joanneum Graz, Landeszeughaus, G 441

69
Conrad Richter, German (1520–1570)
Field Armor of Archduke Karl II of Inner Austria (consisting of helmet, collar, breastplate with tassets, backplate, pauldrons, vambraces, gauntlets, and leg harness with sabatons)
c. 1565
Made in Augsburg
Iron, leather, and brass
Breastplate 39 x 17¾ (99.1 x 45.1)
Joanneum Graz, Landeszeughaus, 1856

70
Martino Rota, Italian (c. 1520–1583)
Portrait of Archduke Karl II of Inner Austria
1576
Engraving on paper, later impression
16 x 12½ (40.5 x 31.6)
Joanneum Graz, Alte Galerie, AK K 5228

71.1
Unidentified artist, after an engraving by Daniel Hefner, Austrian (d. 1624)
Funeral Procession of Karl II of Inner Austria
Unknown date
Oil on paper mounted on canvas
16⅞ x 102⅛ (43 x 259.3)
Joanneum Graz, Alte Galerie, AG 1113

71.2
Unidentified artist, after an engraving by Daniel Hefner, Austrian (d. 1624)
Funeral Procession of Karl II of Inner Austria
Unknown date
Oil on paper mounted on canvas
16 7/8 x 80 3/4 (43 x 205)
Joanneum Graz, Alte Galerie, AG 1114

71.3
Unidentified artist, after an engraving by Daniel Hefner, Austrian (d. 1624)
Funeral Procession of Karl II of Inner Austria
Unknown date
Oil on paper mounted on canvas
16 7/8 x 107 1/4 (43 x 272.3)
Joanneum Graz, Alte Galerie, AG 1115

71.4
Unidentified artist, after an engraving by Daniel Hefner, Austrian (d. 1624)
Funeral Procession of Karl II of Inner Austria
Unknown date
Oil on paper mounted on canvas
16 7/8 x 89 5/8 (43 x 227.6)
Joanneum Graz, Alte Galerie, AG 1116

71.5
Unidentified artist, after an engraving by Daniel Hefner, Austrian (d. 1624)
Funeral Procession of Karl II of Inner Austria
Unknown date
Oil on paper mounted on canvas
16 7/8 x 94 1/2 (43 x 240)
Joanneum Graz, Alte Galerie, AG 1117

71.6
Unidentified artist, after an engraving by Daniel Hefner, Austrian (d. 1624)
Funeral Procession of Karl II of Inner Austria
Unknown date
Oil on paper mounted on canvas
16 7/8 x 37 3/4 (43 x 96)
Joanneum Graz, Alte Galerie, AG 1118

72
Field Armor (consisting of burgonet, almain collar, breastplate with tassets, backplate, vambraces, and gauntlets)
1540–1550
Probably partly made in Innsbruck
Iron and leather
Breastplate 15 x 14 1/8 (38 x 36)
Joanneum Graz, Landeszeughaus, A 2539, A 1610

73
Wolfgang Prenner the Younger, Austrian (d. 1556)
Armor for a Youth
(consisting of helmet, breastplate with tassets, backplate, and almain collar)
c. 1540
Made in Innsbruck
Iron and leather
Breastplate with tassets 24 x 13 1/4 (61 x 33.5)
Joanneum Graz, Landeszeughaus, 1403

74
Sebastian Schmid, Austrian (mentioned 1554–58)
Half Armor for Service on Foot
(consisting of burgonet, almain collar, breastplate with long tassets and codpiece, backplate, and vambraces with gauntlets)
c. 1555
Made in Innsbruck
Iron and leather
Breastplate with tassets 34 1/4 x 16 1/2 (87 x 42)
Joanneum Graz, Landeszeughaus, 1410

75
Two-handed Sword
1530–1540
Made in Styria
Iron, wood, and leather
66 1/8 x 17 3/4 x 5 5/8 (168 x 45 x 14.4)
Joanneum Graz, Landeszeughaus, BL 2

76.1
Armor for an Officer of Infantry or Light Cavalry
1555–60
Probably made in Innsbruck
Russeted iron, brass, and leather
Breastplate 18 1/8 x 15 3/8 (46 x 39)
Joanneum Graz, Landeszeughaus, A 1962

76.2
Helmet for the Armor for an Officer of Infantry or Light Cavalry
1555–60
Probably made in Innsbruck
Russeted iron, brass, and leather
38 x 23 (96.5 x 58.4)
Joanneum Graz, Landeszeughaus, A 1617

77.1
Bodyguard to Count Niklas Zrinyi
c. 1566
Probably made in southern Germany
Woodcut on paper with stenciled color
16 x 10 (40.5 x 25.5)
Joanneum Graz, Alte Galerie, AK. K 10785

77.2
Count Niklas Zrinyi
c. 1566
Probably made in southern Germany
Woodcut on paper with stenciled color
16 x 8½ (40.5 x 21.5)
Joanneum Graz, Alte Galerie, AK. K 10784

77.3
Bodyguard to Count Niklas Zrinyi
c. 1566
Probably made in southern Germany
Woodcut on paper with stenciled color
16 x 10⅞ (40.5 x 27.5)
Joanneum Graz, Alte Galerie, AG. K 10786

78
Landsknecht Hans von Lonispergh
1540
Made in Germany
Walnut
25⅞ x 15⅛ x 2⅞ (65.7 x 38.5 x 7.3)
Joanneum Graz, Abteilung für
Kunstgewerbe, AK 3003

79
Probably the workshop of Georg Lindl,
Austrian (active 1577–1608)
Two-handed Sword
1577–1600
Made in Judenburg
Iron, wood, and leather
70⅛ x 17⅛ x 7⅜ (178 x 43.5 x 18.6)
Joanneum Graz, Landeszeughaus, BL 29

80
Probably the workshop of Georg Lindl,
Austrian (active 1577–1608)
Two-handed Sword
1577–1600
Made in Judenburg
Iron, wood, and leather
67⅛ x 16⅞ x 7⅜ (170.5 x 43 x 18.7)
Joanneum Graz, Landeszeughaus, BL 37

81
Two-handed Sword
1575–1600
Made in Styria
Iron, wood, and leather
69¼ x 20½ x 5⅞ (176 x 52.2 x 15)
Joanneum Graz, Landeszeughaus, BL 49

82
Two-handed Sword
c. 1600
Made in southern Germany
Iron, wood, and leather
74¾ x 19⅜ x 8½ (190 x 49.1 x 21.5)
Joanneum Graz, Landeszeughaus, BL 52

83
Hans Stumpfpöck,
Austrian (active 1589–91)
Two-handed Sword
c. 1590
Made in Weiz, Styria
Iron, wood, leather, and velvet
65¾ x 14⅛ x 7⅞ (167 x 36 x 20)
Joanneum Graz, Landeszeughaus, BL 55

84
Hand-and-a-half Sword
Sixteenth century
Blade made in southern Germany (Passau?);
hilt made in Styria
Iron, wood, and leather
43⅞ x 12¼ x 6¾ (111.5 x 31.2 x 17.2)
Joanneum Graz, Landeszeughaus, BL 9

85
Hand-and-a-half Sword
Sixteenth century
Blade made in southern Germany (Passau?);
hilt made in Styria
Iron, wood, and leather
45⅛ x 16⅜ x 5⅞ (114.5 x 41.5 x 15.1)
Joanneum Graz, Landeszeughaus, BL 10

86
Hand-and-a-half Sword
Sixteenth century
Made in southern Germany (Passau?)
Iron, wood, and leather
42½ x 14⅜ x 5⅛ (108 x 36.6 x 13)
Joanneum Landeszeughaus, BL 11

87
Wheel-lock Gun
Barrel dated 1527
Stock decoration 1570–1580
Made in southern Germany
Iron, ebony veneer and other wood, and
bone
45¼ x 6¾ x 3¼ (115.1 x 17.2 x 8)
Joanneum Graz, Landeszeughaus, RG 2

88
**Two-shot Superimposed-charge Gun
with Double Wheel-lock**
c. 1600
Made in southern Germany
Iron, wood, and stag horn
53⅜ x 8⅛ x 3 (135.5 x 20.7 x 7.7)
Joanneum Graz, Landeszeughaus, RG 64

89
Wheel-lock Pistol
Dated 1566
Probably made in Nuremberg
Iron, wood, and bone
27 x 6½ x 2⅜ (68.6 x 16.4 x 5.9)
Joanneum Graz, Landeszeughaus, RP 254

90
Wheel-lock Pistol
c. 1575
Made in Nuremberg
Iron, wood, and bone
22⅝ x 8 x 2⅞ (57.5 x 20.3 x 7.4)
Joanneum Graz, Landeszeughaus, RP 258

91
Wheel-lock Pistol
c. 1575
Made in southern Germany
Iron, wood, and bone
11⅝ x 6¾ x 2⅞ (47.3 x 17 x 7.1)
Joanneum Graz, Landeszeughaus, RP 262

92
Wheel-lock Pistol
c. 1600
Made in southern Germany
Iron, wood, and bone
18½ x 6⅞ x 2⅞ (47.1 x 17.5 x 7.1)
Joanneum Graz, Landeszeughaus, RP 263

93
Double Holster
End of the sixteenth century
Made in southern Germany
Leather
17⅜ x 6¾ x 7½ (44.1 x 17 x 19)
Joanneum Graz, Landeszeughaus, Z 1797

94
Unidentified artist
Painted after the woodcut by Jost Amman
in Georg Ruxner's *Turnierbuch* from 1566
The Great Tournament in Vienna
c. 1570
Oil on canvas
23⅜ x 40⅛ (59.5 x 102)
Joanneum Graz, Abteilung für
Kunstgewerbe, AK 866

95
Michel Witz the Younger,
Austrian (active 1525–1565)
Black-and-White Three-quarter Armor for a Nobleman
c. 1550
Made in Innsbruck
Iron and leather
22½ x 18¾ (57 x 46.5)
Joanneum Graz, Landeszeughaus, 1414

96.1
Michel Witz the Younger,
Austrian (active 1525–1565)
Elements of a Great Garniture for Field and Tournament of Kaspar Baron Völs-Schenkenberg, consisting of parts for the field armor, lighter field armor *(Harnasch)*, armor for the free tourney *(Freiturnier)* and the tilt *(Plankengestech)*
Dated 1560
Made in Innsbruck
Iron and leather
H. of breastplate 18½ (47)
Joanneum Graz, Landeszeughaus, 1415

96.2
Michel Witz the Younger,
Austrian (active 1525–1565)
Elements of a Great Garniture for Field and Tournament of Kaspar Baron Völs-Schenkenberg, consisting of parts for the field armor, lighter field armor *(Harnasch)*, armor for the free tourney *(Freiturnier)* and the tilt *(Plankengestech)*
Dated 1560
Made in Innsbruck
Iron and leather
H. of breastplate 18½ (47)
Joanneum Graz, Landeszeughaus, 1416

96.3
Michel Witz the Younger,
Austrian (active 1525–1565)
Elements of a Great Garniture for Field and Tournament of Kaspar Baron Völs-Schenkenberg, consisting of parts for the field armor, lighter field armor *(Harnasch)*, armor for the free tourney *(Freiturnier)* and the tilt *(Plankengestech)*
Dated 1560
Made in Innsbruck
Iron and leather
H. of breastplate 18½ (47)
Joanneum Graz, Landeszeughaus, 1417

97
Armor for the *Plankengestech nach Italienischer Art*
1570–1580
Made in Augsburg
Iron and leather
H. of breastplate 15⅜ (39)
Joanneum Graz, Landeszeughaus, 1903

98
Halberd (strong ax-blade and short spike)
1500–1525
Made in Austria
Iron and ash
92⅞ x 12⅜ x 1⅛ (236 x 31.5 x 2.9)
Joanneum Graz, Landeszeughaus, ST 8

99
Halberd (strong ax-blade and short spike)
1500–1525
Made in Austria
Iron and ash
98 x 12¾ x 1¼ (249 x 32.2 x 3.1)
Joanneum Graz, Landeszeughaus, ST 10

100
Halberd (strong ax-blade and short spike)
1500–1525
Made in Austria
Iron and ash
94½ x 12⅝ x 1⅜ (240.2 x 32 x 3.3)
Joanneum Graz, Landeszeughaus, ST 31

101
Halberd (strong ax-blade and short spike)
1500–1525
Made in Austria
Iron and ash
94⅞ x 13¼ x 1¼ (241 x 33.6 x 3)
Joanneum Graz, Landeszeughaus, ST 32

102
Halberd (curved ax-blade and blade-like spike)
c. 1550
Made in Austria
Iron and ash
93⅜ x 12⅛ x 1⅝ (237.3 x 30.6 x 4.2)
Joanneum Graz, Landeszeughaus, ST 2618

103
Halberd (curved ax-blade and blade-like spike)
c. 1550
Made in Austria
Iron and ash
97⅞ x 12¼ x 1½ (248.6 x 31.2 x 3.6)
Joanneum Graz, Landeszeughaus, ST 2619

104
Halberd (curved ax-blade and blade-like spike)
c. 1550
Made in Austria
Iron and ash
97⅝ x 12⅛ x 1⅜ (248.1 x 30.8 x 3.5)
Joanneum Graz, Landeszeughaus, ST 2621

105
Halberd (curved ax-blade and blade-like spike)
c. 1550
Made in Austria
Iron and ash
96⅜ x 12⅞ x 1¾ (244.9 x 32.7 x 4.4)
Joanneum Graz, Landeszeughaus, ST 2620

106
Pankraz Taller, Austrian (d. 1612)
Halberd (small ax-blade and long spike)
1582–86
Made in Hall, Upper Austria
Iron, ash, and brass
109⅝ x 10⅝ x 1½ (278.5 x 26.9 x 3.7)
Joanneum Graz, Landeszeughaus, ST 433

107
Pankraz Taller, Austrian (d. 1612)
Halberd (small ax-blade and long spike)
1582–86
Made in Hall, Upper Austria
Iron, ash, and brass
108⅞ x 10⅜ x 1⅜ (276.4 x 26.3 x 3.4)
Joanneum Graz, Landeszeughaus, ST 434

108
Pankraz Taller, Austrian (d. 1612)
Halberd (small ax-blade and long spike)
1582–86
Made in Hall, Upper Austria
Iron, ash, and brass
106⅝ x 10 x 1¼ (270.7 x 25.4 x 3.2)
Joanneum Graz, Landeszeughaus, ST 435

109
Pankraz Taller, Austrian (d. 1612)
Halberd (small ax-blade and long spike)
1582–86
Made in Hall, Upper Austria
Iron, ash, and brass
102⅝ x 9¾ x 1½ (260.6 x 24.8 x 3.7)
Joanneum Graz, Landeszeughaus, ST 436

110
Pankraz Taller, Austrian (d. 1612)
Halberd (small ax-blade and long spike)
1582–86
Made in Hall, Upper Austria
Iron, ash, and brass
109⅛ x 10⅝ x 1⅜ (277.1 x 27.1 x 3.5)
Joanneum Graz, Landeszeughaus, ST 437

111
Pankraz Taller, Austrian (d. 1612)
Halberd (small ax-blade and long spike)
1582–86
Made in Hall, Upper Austria
Iron, ash, and brass
106⅛ x 9½ x 1¼ (269.6 x 24.2 x 3.2)
Joanneum Graz, Landeszeughaus, ST 438

112
Attributed to Pankraz Taller,
Austrian (d. 1612)
Halberd (small ax-blade and long spike)
1582–86
Made in Hall, Upper Austria
Iron, ash, and brass
$105\frac{1}{8}$ x $12\frac{1}{8}$ x $1\frac{3}{8}$ (267 x 30.6 x 3.6)
Joanneum Graz, Landeszeughaus, ST 439

113
Pankraz Taller, Austrian (d. 1612)
Halberd (small ax-blade and long spike)
1582–86
Made in Hall, Upper Austria
Iron, ash, and brass
$106\frac{1}{2}$ x $10\frac{1}{4}$ x $1\frac{3}{8}$ (270.5 x 25.9 x 3.5)
Joanneum Graz, Landeszeughaus, ST 440

114
Pankraz Taller, Austrian (d. 1612)
Halberd (small ax-blade and long spike)
1582–86
Made in Hall, Upper Austria
Iron, ash, and brass
$105\frac{3}{8}$ x $10\frac{1}{4}$ x $1\frac{1}{4}$ (267.7 x 25.9 x 3)
Joanneum Graz, Landeszeughaus, ST 443

115
Attributed to Pankraz Taller,
Austrian (d. 1612)
Halberd (small ax-blade and long spike)
1582–86
Made in Hall, Upper Austria
Iron, ash, and brass
$100\frac{1}{2}$ x $12\frac{5}{8}$ x $1\frac{1}{2}$ (255.3 x 32 x 3.8)
Joanneum Graz, Landeszeughaus, ST 444

116
Peter Schreckeisen, Austrian (d. c. 1584)
Glaive
c. 1575
Made in Waldneukirchen, Upper Austria
Iron and wood
102 x $5\frac{1}{2}$ x $1\frac{3}{8}$ (259 x 14 x 3.5)
Joanneum Graz, Landeszeughaus, ST 2877

117
Peter Schreckeisen, Austrian (d. c. 1584)
Glaive
c. 1575
Made in Waldneukirchen, Upper Austria
Iron and wood
$101\frac{5}{8}$ x $5\frac{7}{8}$ x $1\frac{3}{4}$ (258 x 15 x 3.2)
Joanneum Graz, Landeszeughaus, ST 2878

118
Peter Schreckeisen, Austrian (d. c. 1584)
Glaive
c. 1575
Made in Waldneukirchen, Upper Austria
Iron and ash
$101\frac{5}{8}$ x $5\frac{1}{2}$ x $1\frac{1}{2}$ (258 x 14 x 3.9)
Joanneum Graz, Landeszeughaus, ST 2879

119
Peter Schreckeisen, Austrian (d. c. 1584)
Glaive
1577–81
Made in Waldneukirchen, Upper Austria
Iron and ash
$101\frac{1}{8}$ x $5\frac{3}{4}$ x $1\frac{3}{8}$ (256.8 x 14.5 x 3.3)
Joanneum Graz, Landeszeughaus, ST 2880

120
Peter Schreckeisen, Austrian (d. c. 1584)
Glaive
1577-81
Made in Waldneukirchen, Upper Austria
Iron, ash, and flax(?)
$103\frac{1}{4}$ x $5\frac{1}{2}$ x $1\frac{3}{8}$ (262.4 x 14 x 3.4)
Joanneum Graz, Landeszeughaus, ST 2881

121
Peter Schreckeisen, Austrian (d. c. 1584)
Glaive
1577–81
Made in Waldneukirchen, Upper Austria
Iron, ash, and flax(?)
$103\frac{7}{8}$ x $4\frac{5}{8}$ x $1\frac{3}{8}$ (263.9 x 11.6 x 3.5)
Joanneum Graz, Landeszeughaus, ST 2882

122
Black-and-White Three-quarter Armor for an Officer of Bodyguards
c. 1575
Made in Nuremberg
Iron and leather
Breastplate $18\frac{1}{8}$ x $15\frac{3}{8}$ (46 x 39)
Joanneum Graz, Landeszeughaus, 478

123
Black-and-White Three-quarter Armor for an Officer of Bodyguards
c. 1575
Made in Nuremberg
Iron and leather
Breastplate $18\frac{1}{8}$ x $15\frac{3}{8}$ (46 x 39)
Joanneum Graz, Landeszeughaus, 479

124.1
Infantry Half Armor
(consisting of breastplate, backplate, almain collar, and tassets)
c. 1578
Made in Nuremberg
Iron and leather
Breastplate 13¾ x 19¾ (35 x 50.3)
Joanneum Graz, Landeszeughaus, 538

124.2
Burgonet
c. 1578
Made in Nuremberg
Iron
11⅜ x 11¼ (29 x 28.5)
Joanneum Graz, Landeszeughaus, 859

125.1
Infantry Half Armor
(consisting of breastplate, backplate, almain collar, and tassets)
c. 1578
Made in Nuremberg
Iron and leather
Breastplate 13¾ x 19¾ (35 x 50.3)
Joanneum Graz, Landeszeughaus, 539

125.2
Burgonet
c. 1578
Made in Nuremberg
Iron and leather
11⅜ x 11¼ (29 x 28.5)
Joanneum Graz, Landeszeughaus, 860

126.1
Infantry Half Armor
(consisting of breastplate, backplate, almain collar, and tassets)
c. 1578
Made in Nuremberg
Iron and leather
Breastplate 13¾ x 19¾ (35 x 50.3)
Joanneum Graz, Landeszeughaus, 543

126.2
Burgonet
c. 1578
Made in Nuremberg
Iron and leather
11⅞ x 11¼ (29 x 28.5)
Joanneum Graz, Landeszeughaus, 861

127.1
Infantry Half Armor
(consisting of breastplate, backplate, almain collar, and tassets)
c. 1578
Made in Nuremberg
Iron and leather
Breastplate 13¾ x 19¾ (35 x 50.3)
Joanneum Graz, Landeszeughaus, 546

127.2
Burgonet
c. 1578
Made in Nuremberg
Iron and leather
11⅞ x 11¼ (29 x 28.5)
Joanneum Graz, Landeszeughaus, 862

128.1
Infantry Half Armor
(consisting of breastplate, backplate, almain collar, and tassets)
c. 1578
Made in Nuremberg
Iron and leather
Breastplate 13¾ x 19¾ (35 x 50.3)
Joanneum Graz, Landeszeughaus, 550

128.2
Burgonet
c. 1578
Made in Nuremberg
Iron, leather, and linen
11⅜ x 11¼ (29 x 28.5)
Joanneum Graz, Landeszeughaus, 863

129.1
Infantry Half Armor
(consisting of breastplate, backplate, almain collar, and tassets)
c. 1578
Made in Nuremberg
Iron and leather
Breastplate 13¾ x 19¾ (35 x 50.3)
Joanneum Graz, Landeszeughaus, 551

129.2
Burgonet
c. 1578
Made in Nuremberg
Iron and leather
11⅜ x 11¼ (29 x 28.5)
Joanneum Graz, Landeszeughaus, 864

130.1
Infantry Half Armor
Late sixteenth century
Made in Augsburg
Iron and leather
Breastplate 16⅛ x 22⅞ (41 x 58)
Joanneum Graz, Landeszeughaus, 1501

130.2
Burgonet
Late sixteenth century
Made in Augsburg
Iron and leather
12¼ x 12 (31 x 30.5)
Joanneum Graz, Landeszeughaus, 1693

131.1
Master "BM"
Infantry Half Armor
Late sixteenth century
Made in Augsburg
Iron and leather
Breastplate 16⅛ x 22⅞ (41 x 58)
Joanneum Graz, Landeszeughaus, 1504

131.2
Burgonet
Late sixteenth century
Made in Augsburg
Iron and leather
12¼ x 12 (31 x 30.5)
Joanneum Graz, Landeszeughaus, 1695

132.1
Master "BM "
Infantry Half Armor
Late sixteenth century
Made in Augsburg
Iron and leather
Breastplate 16⅛ x 22⅞ (41 x 58)
Joanneum Graz, Landeszeughaus, 1505

132.2
Burgonet
Late sixteenth century
Made in Augsburg
Iron and leather
12¼ x 12 (31 x 30.5)
Joanneum Graz, Landeszeughaus, 1697

133.1
Master "BM"
Infantry Half Armor
Late sixteenth century
Made in Augsburg
Iron and leather
Breastplate 16⅛ x 22⅞ (41 x 58)
Joanneum Graz, Landeszeughaus, 1527

133.2
Burgonet
Late sixteenth century
Made in Augsburg
Iron and leather
12¼ x 12 (31 x 30.5)
Joanneum Graz, Landeszeughaus, 1698

134.1
Master "BM"
Infantry Half Armor
Late sixteenth century
Made in Augsburg
Iron and leather
Breastplate 16⅛ x 22⅞ (41 x 58)
Joanneum Graz, Landeszeughaus, 1529

134.2
Burgonet
Late sixteenth century
Made in Augsburg
Iron and leather
12¼ x 12 (31 x 30.5)
Joanneum Graz, Landeszeughaus, 1699

135.1
Probably Hieronymus Ringler the Elder, German (active 1562–1590)
Infantry Half Armor
Late sixteenth century
Made in Augsburg
Breastplate 16⅛ x 22⅞ (41 x 58)
Joanneum Graz, Landeszeughaus, 1544

135.2
Burgonet
Late sixteenth century
Made in Augsburg
Iron and leather
12¼ x 12 (31 x 30.5)
Joanneum Graz, Landeszeughaus, 1700

136
Pike
1582–86
Made in Upper Austria
Iron, ash, and linen
151 x 2¼ x 1⅛ (383.6 x 5.6 x 2.8)
Joanneum Graz, Landeszeughaus, ST 2973

137
Pike
1575–1600
Made in Upper Austria
Iron, ash, and linen
146 x 2¼ x 1⅛ (370.8 x 5.6 x 2.8)
Joanneum Graz, Landeszeughaus, ST 2974

138
Pike
1575–1600
Made in Upper Austria
Iron, ash, and linen
150⅜ x 2⅛ x 1⅛ (381.8 x 5.5 x 2.8)
Joanneum Graz, Landeszeughaus, ST 2975

139
Pike
1575–1600
Made in Upper Austria
Iron, ash, and linen
147 x 2⅜ x 1⅛ (373.4 x 5.8 x 2.7)
Joanneum Graz, Landeszeughaus, ST 2976

140
Pike
1575–1600
Made in Upper Austria
Iron, ash, and linen
151⅜ x 2⅜ x 1⅛ (384.4 x 5.8 x 2.9)
Joanneum Graz, Landeszeughaus, ST 2977

141
Pike
1575–1600
Made in Upper Austria
Iron, ash, and linen
147 x 2⅜ x 1⅛ (373.4 x 5.9 x 2.9)
Joanneum Graz, Landeszeughaus, ST 2978

142
Pike
1575–1600
Made in Upper Austria
Iron, ash, and linen
146½ x 2¼ x 1⅛ (372.1 x 5.7 x 2.9)
Joanneum Graz, Landeszeughaus, ST 2979

143
Pike
1575–1600
Made in Upper Austria
Iron, ash, and linen
148¼ x 2¼ x 1¼ (376.6 x 5.7 x 3)
Joanneum Graz, Landeszeughaus, ST 2981

144
Pike
1575–1600
Made in Upper Austria
Iron, ash, and linen
146⅝ x 2⅜ x 1¼ (372.4 x 5.9 x 3)
Joanneum Graz, Landeszeughaus, ST 2982

145
Pike
1575–1600
Made in Upper Austria
Iron, ash, and linen
148⅛ x 2⅛ x 1⅛ (376.3 x 5.3 x 2.8)
Joanneum Graz, Landeszeughaus, ST 2983

146
Pike
1575–1600
Made in Upper Austria
Iron, ash, and linen
145¾ x 2¼ x 1⅛ (370.5 x 5.7 x 2.9)
Joanneum Graz, Landeszeughaus, ST 2984

147
Pike
1575–1600
Made in Upper Austria
Iron, ash, and linen
145½ x 2¼ x 1⅛ (369.6 x 5.7 x 2.7)
Joanneum Graz, Landeszeughaus, ST 2986

148
Infantry Armor for a Youth
Late sixteenth century
Made in Styria
Iron and leather
12⅜ x 14⅛ (31.5 x 36)
Joanneum Graz, Landeszeughaus, A 1994

149
Archduke Ferdinand of Inner Austria
1600–1610
Made in Inner Austria
Oil on canvas
76⅜ x 38¼ (194 x 97)
Joanneum Graz, Alte Galerie, AG 547

150.1
Burgonet for Light Cavalry Half Armor
1560–1570
Made in Nuremberg
Blackened iron and leather
11½ x 13¾ (29 x 35)
Joanneum Graz, Landeszeughaus, A 587

150.2
Cuirass for Light Cavalry Half Armor
1560–1570
Made in Nuremberg
Blackened iron and leather
Breastplate 16⅛ x 14⅛ (41 x 36)
Joanneum Graz, Landeszeughaus, A 2777

150.3
Almain Collar for Light Cavalry Half Armor
1560–1570
Made in Nuremberg
Blackened iron and leather
H. 5⅞ (15)
Joanneum Graz, Landeszeughaus, A 392

151.1
Burgonet for Light Cavalry Half Armor
1560–1570
Made in Nuremberg
Blackened iron and leather
11½ x 13¾ (29 x 35)
Joanneum Graz, Landeszeughaus, A 588

151.2
Cuirass for Light Cavalry Half Armor
1560–1570
Made in Nuremberg
Blackened iron and leather
Breastplate 16⅛ x 14⅛ (41 x 36)
Joanneum Graz, Landeszeughaus, A 2778

151.3
**Almain Collar for Light Cavalry
Half Armor**
1560–1570
Made in Nuremberg
Blackened iron and leather
H. 5⅞ (15)
Joanneum Graz, Landeszeughaus, 391

152.1
Burgonet for Light Cavalry Half Armor
1560–1570
Made in Nuremberg
Blackened iron and leather
11½ x 13¾ (29 x 35)
Joanneum Graz, Landeszeughaus, A 590

152.2
Cuirass for Light Cavalry Half Armor
1560–1570
Made in Nuremberg
Blackened iron and leather
Breastplate 16⅛ x 14⅛ (41 x 36)
Joanneum Graz, Landeszeughaus, A 2775

152.3
**Almain Collar for Light Cavalry
Half Armor**
1560–1570
Made in Nuremberg
Blackened iron and leather
H. 5⅞ (15)
Joanneum Graz, Landeszeughaus, 393

153.1
Burgonet for Light Cavalry Half Armor
1560–1570
Made in Nuremberg
Blackened iron and leather
11½ x 13¾ (29 x 35)
Joanneum Graz, Landeszeughaus, A 593

153.2
Cuirass for Light Cavalry Half Armor
1560–1570
Made in Nuremberg
Blackened iron and leather
Breastplate 16⅛ x 14⅛ (41 x 36)
Joanneum Graz, Landeszeughaus, A 2774

153.3
**Almain Collar for Light Cavalry
Half Armor**
1560–1570
Made in Nuremberg
Blackened iron and leather
H. 5⅞ (15)
Joanneum Graz, Landeszeughaus, 395

154.1
Burgonet for Light Cavalry Half Armor
1560–1570
Made in Nuremberg
Blackened iron and leather
11½ x 13¾ (29 x 35)
Joanneum Graz, Landeszeughaus, A 595

154.2
Cuirass for Light Cavalry Half Armor
1560–1570
Made in Nuremberg
Blackened iron and leather
Breastplate 16⅛ x 14⅛ (41 x 36)
Joanneum Graz, Landeszeughaus, A 2773

154.3
**Almain Collar for Light Cavalry
Half Armor**
1560–1570
Made in Nuremberg
Blackened iron and leather
H. 5⅞ (15)
Joanneum Graz, Landeszeughaus, A 2268

155.1
Burgonet for Light Cavalry Half Armor
1560–1570
Made in Nuremberg
Blackened iron and leather
11½ x 13¾ (29 x 35)
Joanneum Graz, Landeszeughaus, A 596

155.2
Cuirass for Light Cavalry Half Armor
1560–1570
Made in Nuremberg
Blackened iron and leather
Breastplate 16⅛ x 14⅛ (41 x 36)
Joanneum Graz, Landeszeughaus, A 2776

155.3
Almain Collar for Light Cavalry Half Armor
1560–1570
Made in Nuremberg
Blackened iron and leather
H. $5\frac{7}{8}$ (15)
Joanneum Graz, Landeszeughaus, 397

156
Wheel-lock Pistol
1575–1600
Made in Augsburg
Iron, wood, and bone
$24\frac{7}{8}$ x $8\frac{5}{8}$ x $2\frac{5}{8}$ (63.2 x 21.7 x 6.7)
Joanneum Graz, Landeszeughaus, RP 122

157
Wheel-lock Pistol
1575–1600
Made in Augsburg
Iron, wood, and bone
$23\frac{7}{8}$ x $8\frac{3}{8}$ x $2\frac{5}{8}$ (60.7 x 21.3 x 6.5)
Joanneum Graz, Landeszeughaus, RP 123

158
Thomas Berger, German (active 1575–1600)
Wheel-lock Pistol
1575–1600
Made in Augsburg
Iron, wood, and ebony veneer
20 x $7\frac{5}{8}$ x $2\frac{3}{4}$ (50.8 x 19.3 x 6.8)
Joanneum Graz, Landeszeughaus, RP 99

159
Thomas Berger, German (active 1575–1600)
Wheel-lock Pistol
1575–1600
Made in Augsburg
Iron, wood, and ebony veneer
$19\frac{7}{8}$ x $7\frac{7}{8}$ x $2\frac{3}{4}$ (50.4 x 20.2 x 6.9)
Joanneum Graz, Landeszeughaus, RP 100

160
Wheel-lock Pistol
1575–1600
Made in Augsburg
Iron, wood, and bone
25 x $9\frac{7}{8}$ x $3\frac{1}{8}$ (63.4 x 25 x 7.7)
Joanneum Graz, Landeszeughaus, RP 117

161
Wheel-lock Pistol
1575–1600
Made in Augsburg
Iron, wood, and bone
$24\frac{1}{2}$ x $9\frac{7}{8}$ x 3 (62.2 x 25.2 x 7.6)
Joanneum Graz, Landeszeughaus, RP 118

162
Wheel-lock Pistol
1575–1600
Made in Augsburg
Iron, wood, and stag horn
$20\frac{7}{8}$ x $8\frac{1}{4}$ x $2\frac{3}{4}$ (53 x 21 x 6.9)
Joanneum Graz, Landeszeughaus, RP 13

163
Priming Flask
1575–1600
Made in Augsburg
Iron, wood, and stag horn
Dia. $3\frac{1}{8}$ x $2\frac{1}{8}$ (7.9 x 5.3)
Joanneum Graz, Landeszeughaus, PF 2

164
Cartridge Box
1590–1600
Made in Augsburg
Iron, wood, and stag horn
$4\frac{5}{8}$ x $2\frac{1}{2}$ x $2\frac{7}{8}$ (11.5 x 6.4 x 7.5)
Joanneum Graz, Landeszeughaus, PK 1

165
Spanner
1575–1600
Made in Augsburg
Iron
$5\frac{7}{8}$ x 2 x $\frac{3}{4}$ (15.1 x 5 x 2)
Joanneum Graz, Landeszeughaus, Z 898

166
Combined Spanner, Ramrod, and Flask
1600–1650
Probably made in southern Germany
Iron
$18\frac{7}{8}$ x $2\frac{3}{8}$ x $\frac{1}{2}$ (48 x 5.9 x 1.3)
Joanneum Graz, Landeszeughaus, Z 999

167
Holster
1575–1600
Made in Augsburg
Leather
$18\frac{7}{8}$ x $6\frac{1}{8}$ x $4\frac{3}{8}$ (48 x 15.5 x 11)
Joanneum Graz, Landeszeughaus, Z 1808

168
Wheel-lock Pistol
1570–1590
Made in Augsburg
Iron, wood, and bone
20 x $7\frac{1}{2}$ x $2\frac{5}{8}$ (50.8 x 19 x 6.7)
Joanneum Graz, Landeszeughaus, RP 204

169
Priming Flask
1575–1600
Made in Augsburg
Iron, wood, and bone
Dia. 3⅜ x 2⅛ (8.4 x 5.3)
Joanneum Graz, Landeszeughaus, PF 18

170
Cartridge Box
1575–1600
Perhaps made in Augsburg or northern Germany
Iron, wood, and brass
4¾ x 3⅞ x 2⅞ (11.9 x 9.8 x 7.5)
Joanneum Graz, Landeszeughaus, PK 90

171
Spanner
1575–1600
Made in Augsburg
Iron
6⅝ x 1 x ¾ (16.6 x 2.5 x 1.8)
Joanneum Graz, Landeszeughaus, Z 947

172
Wheel-lock Pistol
1575–1600
Made in Augsburg
Iron, wood, and bone
20⅜ x 8¼ x 2⅞ (51.9 x 21 x 7.5)
Joanneum Graz, Landeszeughaus, RP 213

173
Cartridge Box
1575–1600
Made in Augsburg
Wood, iron, and bone
5⅜ x 3⅝ x 2¾ (13.7 x 9.2 x 6.8)
Joanneum Graz, Landeszeughaus, PK 36

174
Spanner
1575–1600
Made in Augsburg
Iron
6⅜ x 1½ x ¾ (16.1 x 3.8 x 2)
Joanneum Graz, Landeszeughaus, Z 966

175
Combined Match- and Wheel-lock Harquebus
c. 1575
Probably made in Nuremberg
Iron, wood, and bone
35⅝ x 3⅛ x 2¾ (90.5 x 7.9 x 6.9)
Joanneum Graz, Landeszeughaus, RG 10

176
Jost Amman (1539–1591) and
Tobias Stimmer (1539–1584)
Dess Neuwen Kunstbuchs...
1570–1580
Made in Germany
Woodcut on paper
6⅞ x 4⅞ (17.5 x 12.5)
Joanneum Graz, Alte Galerie, AG. K 12205

177.1
Cuirass for a Hussar's Armor
1590–1600
Made in Graz
Iron, brass, and leather
21¼ x 15¾ (54 x 40)
Joanneum Graz, Landeszeughaus, A 354

177.2
Hungarian-style Helmet *(Zischägge)* for a Hussar's Armor
1590–1600
Made in Graz
Iron, brass, and leather
H. 14¼ (36)
Joanneum Graz, Landeszeughaus, A 1596

177.3
Mail Shirt for a Hussar's Armor
1590–1600
Made in Graz
Iron and brass
32¼ x 23⅝ (82 x 60)
Joanneum Graz, Landeszeughaus, PZ 142

178.1
Cuirass for a Hussar's Armor
1590–1600
Made in Graz
Iron, brass, and leather
21¼ x 15¾ (54 x 40)
Joanneum Graz, Landeszeughaus, A 2271

178.2
Hungarian-style Helmet *(Zischägge)* for a Hussar's Armor
1590–1600
Made in Graz
Iron, brass, and leather
H. 14¼ (36)
Joanneum Graz, Landeszeughaus, A 1597

178.3
Mail Shirt for a Hussar's Armor
1590–1600
Made in Graz
Iron and brass
32¼ x 23⅝ (82 x 60)
Joanneum Graz, Landeszeughaus, PZ 139

179.1
Cuirass for a Hussar's Armor
1590–1600
Made in Graz
Iron, brass, and leather
21¼ x 15¾ (54 x 40)
Joanneum Graz, Landeszeughaus, A 2269

179.2
Hungarian-style Helmet *(Zischägge)* for a Hussar's Armor
1590–1600
Made in Graz
Iron, brass, and leather
H. 14¼ (36)
Joanneum Graz, Landeszeughaus, A 1594

179.3
Mail Shirt for a Hussar's Armor
1590–1600
Made in Graz
Iron and brass
27⅛ x 23⅝ (69 x 60)
Joanneum Graz, Landeszeughaus, PZ 143

180.1
Cuirass for a Hussar's Armor
1590–1600
Made in Graz
Iron, brass, and leather
21¼ x 15¾ (54 x 40)
Joanneum Graz, Landeszeughaus, A 2270

180.2
Hungarian-style Helmet *(Zischägge)* for a Hussar's Armor
1590–1600
Made in Graz
Iron, brass, and leather
H. 14¼ (36)
Joanneum Graz, Landeszeughaus, A 1593

180.3
Mail Shirt for a Hussar's Armor
1590–1600
Made in Graz
Iron and brass
32¼ x 23⅝ (82 x 60)
Joanneum Graz, Landeszeughaus, PZ 140

182
Hungarian-style Saber
1575–1600
Probably made in Styria
Iron, wood, and leather
35 x 7⅝ x ⅞ (89 x 19.2 x 2.4)
Joanneum Graz, Landeszeughaus, BL 167

183
Hungarian-style Saber
1575–1600
Probably made in Styria
Iron, wood, leather, and brass
39⅜ x 5⅜ x 1⅛ (99.9 x 13.7 x 2.7)
Joanneum Graz, Landeszeughaus, BL 170

184
Hungarian-style Saber
1575–1600
Probably made in Styria
Iron, wood, leather, and brass
39 x 5¾ x 1⅛ (99.2 x 14.5 x 2.7)
Joanneum Graz, Landeszeughaus, BL 173

185
Hungarian-style Saber
1575–1600
Probably made in Styria
Iron, wood, leather, and brass
34⅝ x 4⅞ x 1⅛ (88.1 x 12.5 x 2.8)
Joanneum Graz, Landeszeughaus, BL 174

186
Estoc with Scabbard
1575–1600
Made in Styria
Iron, wood, and leather
Estoc 48 x 6⅜ x 2¾ (121.8 x 16 x 7)
Scabbard 41¾ x 1¾ x ⅞ (106 x 4.5 x 2.4)
Joanneum Graz, Landeszeughaus, BL 590

187
Estoc
1575–1600
Made in Styria
Iron, wood, and copper
45¼ x 5⅞ x 4⅝ (115.1 x 15 x 11.5)
Joanneum Graz, Landeszeughaus, BL 598

188
Estoc
1575–1600
Made in Styria
Iron, wood, and copper
44⅜ x 6⅜ x 4¼ (112.7 x 16 x 10.6)
Joanneum Graz, Landeszeughaus, BL 605

189
Estoc
1575–1600
Made in Styria
Iron, wood, and leather
43¾ x 6¾ x 2⅞ (111.3 x 17 x 7.5)
Joanneum Graz, Landeszeughaus, BL 619

190
Hans Adam Weissenkircher,
Austrian (1646–1695)
St. Mary and St. Ruprecht Pleading for the Victory of the Christian Weapons over the Turks
1691
Made in Graz
Oil on canvas
92½ x 53⅛ (235 x 135)
Ehrenhausen, Mausoleum of Ruprecht von Eggenberg

191
Attributed to Heinrich De Veerle
(active 1650–1700)
Portrait of Wolf von Eggenberg
c. 1680
Made at the Court of Krumau in southern Bohemia
Oil on canvas
78¾ x 51⅛ (200 x 130)
Ehrenhausen, Mausoleum of Ruprecht von Eggenberg

192
Attributed to Heinrich De Veerle
(active 1650–1700)
Portrait of Ruprecht von Eggenberg
c. 1675–80
Made at the Court of Krumau in southern Bohemia
Oil on canvas
78¾ x 51⅛ (200 x 130)
Ehrenhausen, Mausoleum of Ruprecht von Eggenberg

193
Heinrich Aldegrever,
German (1502–c. 1560)
Ornament with Children
1532
Made in Germany
Engraving on paper
1⅝ x 2⅞ (3.9 x 7.5)
Joanneum Graz, Alte Galerie, AK. K 1236

194
Heinrich Aldegrever,
German (1502–c. 1560)
Ornament with Foliage
1532
Made in Germany
Engraving on paper
2⅛ x 2⅞ (5.2 x 7.1)
Joanneum Graz, Alte Galerie, AK. K 4122

195
Heinrich Aldegrever,
German (1502–c. 1560)
Ornament with Foliage and a Child in the Center
1539
Made in Germany
Engraving on paper
1⅜ x 3⅝ (3.5 x 9.1)
Joanneum Graz, Alte Galerie, AK. K 4133

196
Heinrich Aldegrever,
German (1502–c. 1560)
Ornament with Children
1549
Made in Germany
Engraving on paper
1⅝ x 3⅞ (4 x 9.6)
Joanneum Graz, Alte Galerie, AK. K 4135

197
Heinrich Aldegrever,
German (1502–c. 1560)
Ornament with Vase and Mask
1552
Made in Germany
Engraving on paper
5¾ x 2⅛ (14.6 x 5.3)
Joanneum Graz, Alte Galerie, AK. K 1228

198
Heinrich Aldegrever,
German (1502–c. 1560)
Ornament Arising from the Body of a Faun
1552
Made in Germany
Engraving on paper
5½ x 1¾ (14 x 4.5)
Joanneum Graz, Alte Galerie, AK. K 1229

199
Abraham de Bruyn, Dutch (1540–c. 1587)
Perseus
1584
Engraving on paper
3½ x 4⅞ (8.7 x 12.4)
Joanneum Graz, Alte Galerie, AK. K 2921

200
Abraham de Bruyn, Dutch (1540–c. 1587)
Phineus
1584
Engraving on paper
3½ x 4⅞ (8.9 x 12.3)
Joanneum Graz, Alte Galerie, AG. K 2922

201
Virgil Solis, German (1514–1562)
Joshua (from a series of the *Nine Worthies*)
Early 1550s
Made in Germany
Engraving on paper
3½ x 2⅜ (8.8 x 6)
Joanneum Graz, Alte Galerie, AK. K 2692

202
Virgil Solis, German (1514–1562)
Julius Caesar (from a series of the *Nine Worthies*)
Early 1550s
Made in Germany
Engraving on paper
3½ x 2⅜ (8.7 x 5.9)
Joanneum Graz, Alte Galerie, AK. K 2697

203
Virgil Solis, German (1514–1562)
King Arthur (from a series of the *Nine Worthies*)
Early 1550s
Made in Germany
Engraving on paper
3½ x 2⅜ (8.8 x 6)
Joanneum Graz, Alte Galerie, AK. K 2699

204
Christoph Jamnitzer, German (1563–1618)
Ornamental (Moresque) Band with Initials M A
1610
Made in Germany
Engraving on paper
1⅝ x 6⅝ (3.9 x 16.8)
Joanneum Graz, Alte Galerie, AK. K 2336

205
Christoph Jamnitzer, German (1563–1618)
Ornamental (Moresque) Band with Woman's Head
1610
Made in Germany
Engraving on paper
1⅜ x 6½ (3.4 x 16.5)
Joanneum Graz, Alte Galerie, AG. K 2340

206
Master "MR" (perhaps Martin Rotschmied, Michel Roth, or Martin Rotschuch)
Morion
c. 1575
Made in Nuremberg
Etched and blackened iron
13⅛ x 14⅝ (33.5 x 37)
Joanneum Graz, Landeszeughaus, 1280

207
Close Helmet for the Field
1550–1575
Made in Nuremberg
Iron and leather
13¾ x 14 (35 x 35.5)
Joanneum Graz, Landeszeughaus, 1273

208
Cuirass with Tassets
1550–1575
Made in southern Germany
Iron and leather
Breastplate 26⅜ x 13 (67 x 33)
Joanneum Graz, Landeszeughaus, A 2590

209
Unidentified artist
Star-like mark stamped on blade near hilt
Ceremonial Sword
c. 1600
Blade possibly made in Italy; hilt made in southern Germany or Styria
Steel, wood, gilt enamel, and textile
46 x 9⅝ x 3⅛ (117 x 24.5 x 8)
Joanneum Graz, Abteilung für Kunstgewerbe, AK 822

210
Boar Spear
1573
Made in Styria
Iron, wood, leather, and flax(?)
L. 81⅝ (207.3)
Joanneum Graz, Landeszeughaus, ST 5395

211
Glaive for the Guard of Archduke Sigismund Franz of Tyrol
1663
Made in southern Germany or Austria
Iron and wood
95⅜ x 3⅛ x 1⅝ (242.4 x 7.8 x 3.9)
Joanneum Graz, Landeszeughaus, ST 2924

212
Halberd
Late sixteenth century
Made in Upper Austria
Iron, wood, leather, and velvet
89⅛ x 8⅛ x 1⅝ (226.3 x 20.5 x 4.1)
Joanneum Graz, Landeszeughaus, ST 2697

213
Halberd
Late sixteenth century
Probably made in Upper Austria
Iron, wood, leather, and velvet
79¼ x 9¾ x 1⅝ (201.2 x 24.6 x 3.9)
Joanneum Graz, Landeszeughaus, ST 2695

214
Halberd
Late sixteenth century
Probably made in Upper Austria
Iron, wood, and velvet
$86\frac{3}{4}$ x $8\frac{1}{4}$ x $1\frac{3}{4}$ (220.4 x 21 x 4.3)
Joanneum Graz, Landeszeughaus, ST 2698

215
Ceremonial Partisan for the Guard of Hans Franz von Stainach
1628
Made in southern Germany or Styria
Iron, silver, brass, ash, and silk
$98\frac{1}{4}$ x $9\frac{5}{8}$ x 6 (249.4 x 24.5 x 15.2)
Joanneum Graz, Landeszeughaus, ST 2931

216
Barrelmaker: Master "IP"
Stockmaker: Master "HM"
Double-barreled, Double Wheel-lock Pistol
c. 1580
Made in southern Germany
Iron, wood, and bone
$22\frac{1}{2}$ x $7\frac{7}{8}$ x $2\frac{7}{8}$ (57.2 x 20.2 x 7.5)
Joanneum Graz, Landeszeughaus, RP 158

217
Wheel-lock Pistol
c. 1575
Made in Nuremberg
Iron, wood, and bone
23 x $8\frac{5}{8}$ x $2\frac{7}{8}$ (58.4 x 22 x 7.2)
Joanneum Graz, Landeszeughaus, RP 189

218
Wheel-lock Pistol
c. 1575
Made in Nuremberg
Iron, wood, and bone
23 x 8 x $2\frac{7}{8}$ (58.4 x 20.3 x 7.1)
Joanneum Graz, Landeszeughaus, RP 190

219.1
Nikolaus Klett, German (active 1591–1608)
Wheel-lock Pistol (one of a pair)
c. 1610
Made in Suhl-Henneberg, Thuringia
Iron, wood, and bone
$30\frac{1}{2}$ x $6\frac{1}{4}$ x $2\frac{3}{8}$ (77.5 x 15.9 x 6)
Joanneum Graz, Landeszeughaus, RP 285

219.2
Nikolaus Klett, German (active 1591–1608)
Wheel-lock Pistol (one of a pair)
c. 1610
Made in Suhl-Henneberg, Thuringia
Iron, wood, and bone
$30\frac{1}{2}$ x $4\frac{7}{8}$ x $2\frac{1}{2}$ (77.5 x 12.5 x 6.2)
Joanneum Graz, Landeszeughaus, RP 286

220
Combined Match- and Wheel-lock Musket
c. 1600
Made in Augsburg
Iron, wood, and bone
$51\frac{1}{8}$ x $9\frac{5}{8}$ x $3\frac{1}{2}$ (129.7 x 24.5 x 8.8)
Joanneum Graz, Landeszeughaus, RG 47

221
Wheel-lock Musket
c. 1600
Made in Augsburg
Iron, wood, and bone
$54\frac{1}{2}$ x $9\frac{3}{4}$ x $3\frac{1}{4}$ (138.3 x 24.7 x 8.1)
Joanneum Graz, Landeszeughaus, RG 48

222
Wheel-lock Musket
c. 1600
Made in Augsburg
Iron, wood, and bone
57 x $10\frac{5}{8}$ x 4 (144.9 x 27 x 10.1)
Joanneum Graz, Landeszeughaus, RG 67

223
Nikolaus Karpf,
German (active c. 1590–1600)
Wheel-lock Harquebus
c. 1590–1600
Made in Augsburg
Iron, wood, and bone
$32\frac{3}{4}$ x $8\frac{3}{8}$ x $3\frac{1}{2}$ (83.3 x 21.2 x 8.8)
Joanneum Graz, Landeszeughaus, RP 266

224.1
Sporting Crossbow
1550–1600
Probably made in Austria
Iron, rosewood, bone, and hemp
$24\frac{5}{8}$ x $24\frac{3}{4}$ x $2\frac{7}{8}$ (62.6 x 63 x 7.4)
Joanneum Graz, Abteilung für Kunstgewerbe, AK 1142

224.2
Winder for a Crossbow
1550–1600
Made in southern Germany or Austria
Iron, wood, bone, and hemp
$13\frac{5}{8}$ x $9\frac{1}{2}$ x $3\frac{1}{8}$ (34.5 x 24 x 7.8)
Joanneum Graz, Abteilung für Kunstgewerbe, AK 1142

224.3
Crossbow Bolt
1550–1600
Made in southern Germany or Austria
Iron and wood
$14\frac{3}{8}$ x 1 x $\frac{3}{8}$ (36.4 x 2.6 x .9)
Joanneum Graz, Abteilung für Kunstgewerbe, SW 548

225
Stock for a Hunting Rifle
1600–1625
Probably made in southern Germany
Wood, bone, iron, and gilt
54⅝ x 13¾ x 3⅜ (138.8 x 35 x 8.6)
Joanneum Graz, Landeszeughaus, RG 1026

226
Stockmaker: Master "ND"
Wheel-lock Hunting Rifle
c. 1580
Made in southern Germany
Iron, wood, bone, and gilt
44⅝ x 7⅛ x 3⅛ (113.3 x 18 x 7.9)
Joanneum Graz, Landeszeughaus, RG 1024

227
Barrelmaker: Master "MM"
Stockmaker: Master "CO"
Wheel-lock Hunting Rifle
c. 1600
Made in southern Germany
Iron, wood, bone, and gilt
46¼ x 7⅞ x 3½ (117.4 x 20 x 8.7)
Joanneum Graz, Landeszeughaus, RG 1025

228
Cartridge Box
c. 1600
Made in southern Germany
Wood, bone, and iron
4½ x 2¾ x 2⅝ (11.3 x 6.9 x 6.6)
Joanneum Graz, Landeszeughaus, PK 12

229
Cartridge Box
1580–1590
Made in southern Germany
Wood, bone, and iron
4⅝ x 1⅞ x 2⅜ (11.7 x 4.7 x 5.8)
Joanneum Graz, Landeszeughaus, PK 16

230
Cartridge Box
1580–1590
Made in southern Germany
Wood, bone, and iron
4⅞ x 2⅝ x 2¾ (12.4 x 6.5 x 7)
Joanneum Graz, Landeszeughaus, PK 18

231
Cartridge Box
c. 1600
Made in southern Germany
Wood, bone, brass, and iron
5⅛ x 3¾ x 2½ (12.9 x 9.3 x 6.3)
Joanneum Graz, Landeszeughaus, PK 19

232
Cartridge Box
1580–1590
Made in southern Germany or Brunswick
Iron, wood, and brass
4¾ x 3⅞ x 2¾ (11.9 x 9.9 x 6.8)
Joanneum Graz, Landeszeughaus, PK 83

233
Philips Wouwerman, Dutch (1619–1668)
Soldiers in Baggage Train
c. 1650
Probably made in Haarlem
Oil on wood
13 x 15¾ (33 x 40)
Joanneum Graz, Alte Galerie, AG 118

234
Jacob Jacques de Gheyn,
Dutch (1565–1629)
Waffenhandlung von den Rören, Musquetten undt Spiessen
1607
Made in Amsterdam
Engraving on paper
12⅞ x 19⅛ (32.5 x 48.5)
Joanneum Graz, Landeszeughaus, IV 12702

235
Matchlock Musket
1600–1620
Made in Suhl-Henneberg, Thuringia
Iron and wood
60½ x 8½ x 2⅝ (153.8 x 21.5 x 6.6)
Joanneum Graz, Landeszeughaus, LG 554

236
Musket Rest
1600–1650
Probably made in Styria
Wood and iron
56 x 2⅞ x ⅞ (142.3 x 7.2 x 2)
Joanneum Graz, Landeszeughaus, Z 386

237
Bandoleer
Seventeenth century
Probably made in Styria
Wood, leather, parchment, and hide
L. of pendant 5⅜ (13.5)
Joanneum Graz, Landeszeughaus, PF 2894

238
Wheel-lock Harquebus
c. 1590
Made in Augsburg
Iron, wood, and bone
31⅛ x 8⅛ x 3¼ (79 x 20.6 x 8.3)
Joanneum Graz, Landeszeughaus, RG 267

239
Powder Flask
1600–1650
Made in Styria
Wood and iron
9¼ x 4⅝ x 1⅞ (23.5 x 11.8 x 4.7)
Joanneum Graz, Landeszeughaus, PF 1270

240
Marksman's Helmet
1577–78
Made in Nuremberg
Iron and leather
14⅛ x 7½ (36 x 19)
Joanneum Graz, Landeszeughaus, 980

241.1
Hans Prenner, Austrian (d. 1645)
Infantry Half Armor (consisting of breastplate, backplate, collar, and tassets)
1615–1631
Made in Graz
Iron and leather
Breastplate 15¾ x 14⅛ (40 x 36)
Joanneum Graz, Landeszeughaus, A 1973

241.2
Hans Prenner, Austrian (d. 1645)
Burgonet for Infantry Half Armor
1615–1631
Made in Graz
Iron and leather
12⅝ x 13¾ (32 x 35)
Joanneum Graz, Landeszeughaus, A 676

242.1
Hans Prenner, Austrian (d. 1645)
Infantry Half Armor (consisting of breastplate, backplate, collar, and tassets)
1615–1631
Made in Graz
Iron and leather
Breastplate 15¾ x 14⅛ (40 x 36)
Joanneum Graz, Landeszeughaus, A 1974

242.2
Hans Prenner, Austrian (d. 1645)
Burgonet for Infantry Half Armor
1615–1631
Made in Graz
Iron and leather
12⅝ x 13¾ (32 x 35)
Joanneum Graz, Landeszeughaus, A 648

243.1
Hans Prenner, Austrian (d. 1645)
Infantry Half Armor (consisting of breastplate, backplate, collar, and tassets)
1615–1631
Made in Graz
Iron and leather
Breastplate 15¾ x 14⅛ (40 x 36)
Joanneum Graz, Landeszeughaus, A 1975

243.2
Hans Prenner, Austrian (d. 1645)
Burgonet for Infantry Half Armor
1615–1631
Made in Graz
Iron and leather
12⅝ x 13¾ (32 x 35)
Joanneum Graz, Landeszeughaus, A 649

244.1
Hans Prenner, Austrian (d. 1645)
Infantry Half Armor (consisting of breastplate, backplate, collar, and tassets)
1615–1631
Made in Graz
Iron and leather
Breastplate 15¾ x 14⅛ (40 x 36)
Joanneum Graz, Landeszeughaus, A 1976

244.2
Hans Prenner, Austrian (d. 1645)
Burgonet for Infantry Half Armor
1615–1631
Made in Graz
Iron and leather
12⅝ x 13¾ (32 x 35)
Joanneum Graz, Landeszeughaus, A 650

245.1
Hans Prenner, Austrian (d. 1645)
Infantry Half Armor (consisting of breastplate, backplate, collar, and tassets)
1615–1631
Made in Graz
Iron and leather
Breastplate 15¾ x 14⅛ (40 x 36)
Joanneum Graz, Landeszeughaus, A 1977

245.2
Hans Prenner, Austrian (d. 1645)
Burgonet for Infantry Half Armor
1615–1631
Made in Graz
Iron and leather
12⅝ x 13¾ (32 x 35)
Joanneum Graz, Landeszeughaus, A 651

246.1
Hans Prenner, Austrian (d. 1645)
Infantry Half Armor (consisting of breastplate, backplate, collar, and tassets)
1615–1631
Made in Graz
Iron and leather
Breastplate 15¾ x 14⅛ (40 x 36)
Joanneum Graz, Landeszeughaus, A 1978

246.2
Hans Prenner, Austrian (d. 1645)
Burgonet for Infantry Half Armor
1615–1631
Made in Graz
Iron and leather
12⅝ x 13¾ (32 x 35)
Joanneum Graz, Landeszeughaus, A 652

247.1
Hans Prenner, Austrian (d. 1645)
Infantry Half Armor (consisting of breastplate, backplate, collar, and tassets)
1615–1631
Made in Graz
Iron and leather
Breastplate 15¾ x 14⅛ (40 x 36)
Joanneum Graz, Landeszeughaus, A 1965

247.2
Hans Prenner, Austrian (d. 1645)
Burgonet for Infantry Half Armor
1615–1631
Made in Graz
Iron and leather
12⅝ x 13¾ (32 x 35)
Joanneum Graz, Landeszeughaus, A 637

248.1
Hans Prenner, Austrian (d. 1645)
Infantry Half Armor (consisting of breastplate, backplate, collar, and tassets)
1615–1631
Made in Graz
Iron and leather
Breastplate 15¾ x 14⅛ (40 x 36)
Joanneum Graz, Landeszeughaus, A 1966

248.2
Hans Prenner, Austrian (d. 1645)
Burgonet for Infantry Half Armor
1615–1631
Made in Graz
Iron and leather
12⅝ x 13¾ (32 x 35)
Joanneum Graz, Landeszeughaus, A 638

249.1
Hans Prenner, Austrian (d. 1645)
Infantry Half Armor (consisting of breastplate, backplate, collar, and tassets)
1615–1631
Made in Graz
Iron and leather
Breastplate 15¾ x 14⅛ (40 x 36)
Joanneum Graz, Landeszeughaus, A 1967

249.2
Hans Prenner, Austrian (d. 1645)
Burgonet for Infantry Half Armor
1615–1631
Made in Graz
Iron and leather
12⅝ x 13¾ (32 x 35)
Joanneum Graz, Landeszeughaus, A 639

250.1
Hans Prenner, Austrian (d. 1645)
Infantry Half Armor (consisting of breastplate, backplate, collar, and tassets)
1615–1631
Made in Graz
Iron and leather
Breastplate 15¾ x 14⅛ (40 x 36)
Joanneum Graz, Landeszeughaus, A 1968

250.2
Hans Prenner, Austrian (d. 1645)
Burgonet for Infantry Half Armor
1615–1631
Made in Graz
Iron and leather
12⅝ x 13¾ (32 x 35)
Joanneum Graz, Landeszeughaus, A 640

251.1
Hans Prenner, Austrian (d. 1645)
Infantry Half Armor (consisting of breastplate, backplate, collar, and tassets)
1615–1631
Made in Graz
Iron and leather
Breastplate 15¾ x 14⅛ (40 x 36)
Joanneum Graz, Landeszeughaus, A 1969

251.2
Hans Prenner, Austrian (d. 1645)
Burgonet for Infantry Half Armor
1615–1631
Made in Graz
Iron and leather
12⅝ x 13¾ (32 x 35)
Joanneum Graz, Landeszeughaus, A 641

252.1
Hans Prenner, Austrian (d. 1645)
Infantry Half Armor (consisting of breastplate, backplate, collar, and tassets)
1615–1631
Made in Graz
Iron and leather
Breastplate 15¾ x 14⅛ (40 x 36)
Joanneum Graz, Landeszeughaus, A 1971

252.2
Hans Prenner, Austrian (d. 1645)
Burgonet for Infantry Half Armor
1615–1631
Made in Graz
Iron and leather
12⅝ x 13¾ (32 x 35)
Joanneum Graz, Landeszeughaus, A 642

253
Pike
1550–1600
Probably made in Upper Austria
Iron and ash
102½ x 1½ x 1¼ (260.3 x 3.6 x 3)
Joanneum Graz, Landeszeughaus, ST 3426

254
Pike
1550–1600
Probably made in Upper Austria
Iron and ash
101¼ x 1⅝ x 1¼ (257.1 x 4 x 3.2)
Joanneum Graz, Landeszeughaus, ST 3427

255
Pike
1550–1600
Probably made in Upper Austria
Iron and ash
100⅛ x 1⅝ x 1¼ (254.3 x 4 x 3.1)
Joanneum Graz, Landeszeughaus, ST 3428

256
Pike
1550–1600
Probably made in Upper Austria
Iron and ash
101⅛ x 1⅝ x 1¼ (256.8 x 4.1 x 3)
Joanneum Graz, Landeszeughaus, ST 3429

257
Pike
1550–1600
Probably made in Upper Austria
Iron and ash
99¾ x 1⅝ x 1⅛ (253.4 x 3.9 x 2.9)
Joanneum Graz, Landeszeughaus, ST 3430

258
Pike
1550–1600
Probably made in Upper Austria
Iron and ash
106⅝ x 1⅝ x 1¼ (270.8 x 3.9 x 3.1)
Joanneum Graz, Landeszeughaus, ST 3431

259
Pike
1550–1600
Probably made in Upper Austria
Iron and ash
102½ x 1⅝ x 1¼ (260.2 x 4.1 x 3.1)
Joanneum Graz, Landeszeughaus, ST 3432

260
Pike
1550–1600
Probably made in Upper Austria
Iron and ash
99⅛ x 1⅝ x 1⅛ (251.6 x 4.1 x 2.9)
Joanneum Graz, Landeszeughaus, ST 3433

261
Pike
1550–1600
Made in Upper Austria
Iron and ash
101¾ x 1½ x 1⅛ (258.5 x 3.8 x 2.9)
Joanneum Graz, Landeszeughaus, ST 3434

262
Pike
1550–1600
Probably made in Upper Austria
Iron and ash
99⅜ x 1½ x 1⅜ (252.4 x 3.8 x 3.3)
Joanneum Graz, Landeszeughaus, ST 3435

263
Pike
1550–1600
Probably made in Upper Austria
Iron and ash
100 x 1⅝ x 1⅜ (254 x 4.1 x 3.3)
Joanneum Graz, Landeszeughaus, ST 3436

264
Pike
1550–1600
Probably made in Upper Austria
Iron and ash
101⅜ x 1⅝ x 1¼ (257.4 x 4 x 3.2)
Joanneum Graz, Landeszeughaus, ST 3437

265
Rondache
c. 1610
Made in Nuremberg
Iron, brass, and leather
Dia. 21⅝ x 4⅝ (55 x 11.5)
Joanneum Graz, Landeszeughaus, 1186

266
Rondache
c. 1610
Made in Nuremberg
Iron, brass, and leather
Dia. 22⅜ x 4⅛ (57 x 10.4)
Joanneum Graz, Landeszeughaus, 1196

267
Rondache
c. 1610
Made in Nuremberg
Iron and brass
Dia. 22 1/16 x 3⅜ (56 x 8.4)
Joanneum Graz, Landeszeughaus, 1198

268
Rondache
c. 1610
Made in Nuremberg
Iron, brass, and leather
Dia. 24 x 4⅜ (61 x 11)
Joanneum Graz, Landeszeughaus, 1199

269
Rondache
c. 1610
Made in Nuremberg
Iron and brass
Dia. 24 x 3⅛ (61 x 7.7)
Joanneum Graz, Landeszeughaus, 1202

270
Rondache
c. 1610
Made in Nuremberg
Iron and brass
Dia. 22⅞ x 4⅛ (58 x 10.5)
Joanneum Graz, Landeszeughaus, 1205

271
Attributed to Hans Prenner,
Austrian (d. 1645)
Three-quarter Armor for Heavy Cavalry
c. 1620
Made in Graz
Iron, brass, and leather
Breastplate 16⅛ x 13⅞ (41 x 35.2)
Joanneum Graz, Landeszeughaus, A 2568

272
Attributed to Hans Prenner,
Austrian (d. 1645)
Three-quarter Armor for Heavy Cavalry
c. 1600
Made in Graz
Iron, brass, and leather
Breastplate 16⅛ x 13⅞ (41 x 35.2)
Joanneum Graz, Landeszeughaus, A 2575

273
Attributed to Hans Prenner,
Austrian (d. 1645)
Three-quarter Armor for Heavy Cavalry
c. 1620
Made in Graz
Iron, brass, and leather
Breastplate 16⅛ x 13⅞ (41 x 35.2)
Joanneum Graz, Landeszeughaus, A 2577

274
Attributed to Hans Prenner,
Austrian (d. 1645)
Three-quarter Armor for Heavy Cavalry
c. 1635
Made in Graz
Iron and leather
Breastplate 16⅛ x 13⅞ (41 x 35.2)
Joanneum Graz, Landeszeughaus, A 2583

275
Attributed to Hans Prenner,
Austrian (d. 1645)
Three-quarter Armor for Heavy Cavalry
c. 1635
Made in Graz
Iron and leather
Breastplate 16⅛ x 13⅞ (41 x 35.2)
Joanneum Graz, Landeszeughaus, A 2584

276
Attributed to Hans Prenner,
Austrian (d. 1645)
Three-quarter Armor for Heavy Cavalry
c. 1635
Made in Graz
Iron and leather
Breastplate 16⅛ x 13⅞ (41 x 35.2)
Joanneum Graz, Landeszeughaus, A 2586

277
Attributed to Hans Prenner,
Austrian (d. 1645)
Three-quarter Armor for Heavy Cavalry
c. 1635
Iron and leather
Breastplate 16⅛ x 13⅞ (41 x 35.2)
Joanneum Graz, Landeszeughaus, A 2587

278
Wheel-lock Pistol
c. 1620
Made in Augsburg
Iron, wood, and brass
27¾ x 5¾ x 2⅞ (70.5 x 14.6 x 7.3)
Joanneum Graz, Landeszeughaus, RP 276

279
Wheel-lock Pistol
c. 1620
Made in Augsburg
Iron, wood, brass, and bone
26 x 5½ x 3 (65.8 x 14 x 7.5)
Joanneum Graz, Landeszeughaus, RP 277

280
Sword
1580–1620
Made in Passau
Iron, wood, and leather
51⅜ x 13½ x 7⅝ (130.5 x 34.2 x 19.2)
Joanneum Graz, Landeszeughaus, BL 15

281
Sword
1580–1620
Made in Styria
Iron, wood, and fish skin
45⅝ x 14 x 7⅛ (116 x 35.5 x 18)
Joanneum Graz, Landeszeughaus, BL 18

282
Sword
1580–1620
Made in Styria
Iron, wood, and fish skin
41⅛ x 14 x 7¾ (104.5 x 35.5 x 19.5)
Joanneum Graz, Landeszeughaus, BL 19

283
Cavalry Sword
c. 1570–80
Probably made in southern Germany
Iron, wood, and leather
49¾ x 8⅛ x 5⅛ (126.5 x 20.5 x 13)
Joanneum Graz, Landeszeughaus, BL 8

284
Cavalry Sword
c. 1570–80
Made in Styria
Iron, wood, and leather
37⅝ x 14½ x 6¼ (95.5 x 37 x 16)
Joanneum Graz, Landeszeughaus, BL 12

285
Cavalry Sword
c. 1570–80
Made in Styria
Iron, wood, and brass
43⅛ x 5⅛ x 5⅛ (109.4 x 13 x 13)
Joanneum Graz, Landeszeughaus, BL 16

286
Cavalry Sword
c. 1580–90
Made in Styria
Iron, wood, and leather
46 x 13 x 5½ (117 x 33 x 14)
Joanneum Graz, Landeszeughaus, BL 20

287
Strong Box for Military Funds
1600–1650
Iron
21⅝ x 48⅜ x 24 (55 x 123 x 61)
Joanneum Graz, Abteilung für
Kunstgewerbe, AK 1317

288
Attributed to workshop of Conrad Seiser,
Austrian (d. 1654)
Mortar
c. 1650
Made in Styria
Bronze and oak
Mortar 20½ (50)
Barrel 17¾ x 8¾ (45 x 22.3)
Joanneum Graz, Landeszeughaus, G 387

289
The Battle of Mogersdorf
c. 1665
Made in southern Germany
Oil on canvas
68½ x 102⅜ (174 x 260)
Schloss Obermurau,
Prinz K. Schwarzenberg

REIGNS OF HOLY ROMAN
AND OTTOMAN EMPERORS

HOLY ROMAN EMPIRE

Frederick III	reigned 1452–1493
Maximilian I	reigned 1493–1519
Charles V	reigned 1519–1556
Ferdinand I	reigned 1556–1564
Maximilian II	reigned 1564–1576
Rudolph II	reigned 1576–1612
Mattias	reigned 1612–1619
Ferdinand II	reigned 1619–1637
Ferdinand III	reigned 1637–1657
Leopold I	reigned 1658–1705

OTTOMAN EMPIRE

Murad II	reigned 1421–1444; 1446–1451
Mehmed II	reigned 1444–1446; 1451–1481
Bayazid	reigned 1481–1512
Selim I	reigned 1512–1520
Süleyman I the Magnificent	reigned 1520–1566
Selim II "The Sot"	reigned 1566–1574
Murad III	reigned 1574–1595
Mehmed III	reigned 1595–1603
Ahmed I	reigned 1603–1617
Mustafa I	reigned 1617–1618; 1622–1623
Osman II	reigned 1618–1622
Murad IV	reigned 1623–1640
Ibrahim I	reigned 1640–1648
Mehmed IV	reigned 1648–1687
Süleyman II	reigned 1687–1691
Ahmed II	reigned 1691–1695
Mustafa II	reigned 1695–1703

INDEX OF ARTISTS, ARMORERS, AND ARMS DECORATORS

133

Photography by Bild und Tonarchiv Graz [figures 8–10]; Lynn Diane DeMarco [figures 15, 38, 43–46, 85, 86]; Reinhart Dittrich [figures 47, 59]; Foto Fürböck [figure 52]; Richard Margolis [Cover (checklist no. 95), figures 1, 4, 16, 18, 23–26, 28, 33, 34, 37, 39, 40, 49, 51, 53, 55, 61, 62, 65, 67, 73, 75, 87, 89, 94, 95]; Michael Oberer [Cover (checklist nos. 274–277), figures 12, 29, 41, 48, 54, 58, 68, 69, 76, 77, 83, 88, 90, 91]; Stadtmuseum Graz [figure 56]; Verlag Hofstetter [figures 6, 27, 57, 84]; Hans Wiesenhofer [figure 35]; and Matthias Wimler [Frontisepiece, figures 2, 3, 5, 7, 11, 13, 14, 17, 19–22, 30–32, 36, 42, 50, 60, 63, 64, 66, 70–72, 74, 78–82, 92, 93, 96].